C000163363

1

Divorcing and Co-parenting with a Narcissist:

How to protect your kids from your Ex Spouse by divorcing and Healing from a Narcissistic Ex Partner.

Recover from Emotional Abuse in toxic relationships.

AMANDA LYNN

Table of Contents

Introduction

Many people know the term narcissism comes from the tale of Narcissus, the Greek youth who fell in love with his own reflection. Still, many are unsure how to identify narcissism, and perhaps most importantly, how to live with it when the disorder has an effect on them. What's important to first understand is that, unlike the handsome and vain Narcissus, a true narcissist doesn't really love himself; rather, he suffers from a lack of an authentic self.

People who tend toward narcissistic personality disorder (NPD) did not develop a healthy sense of self-esteem at a critical age. Whether the fault of caregivers who were unable to provide "empathetic attunement" to their young child, or the result of another trauma, the consequences are that narcissists believe they must be beautiful, smart, talented, and admired. Narcissists are often high-achieving individuals who possess a constant need to prove themselves to gain love—and to compensate for the lack of it in their childhood. As children, many people with NPD had to present an image of perfection, beauty, and success. As a result, they wear the mask of a false self, afraid others will perceive these feelings of inadequacy through their disguise.

No matter how difficult those with NPD may be to relate to, it's important to note that the dynamics resulting in troublesome behaviors, such as the constant need for admiration and assurance, the lack of empathy, and the arrogance and vanity, are simply unconscious attempts to maintain a false self. After feeling that their true thoughts and feelings didn't matter, narcissists may fear for their psychological survival and become preoccupied with having their needs met and their feelings understood or "mirrored."

When you understand the roots of NPD, you can learn to alter the dynamics of a difficult relationship between yourself and someone who exhibits narcissistic tendencies. In this book, you'll gain tools to transform your relationships, with the goal that you can become your own advocate, rather than try to change the narcissist. While the natural tendency may be to confront a narcissist about their offending behavior, this tactic has poor results and reinforces the narcissist's feelings of victimization. The best strategy is to make the narcissist feel wanted and appreciated. Meeting negativity with more negativity fuels the narcissist's need to defend. Instead, defuse the interaction by acting on insight and attempt to make your own needs known in a calm, nonconfrontational way. When dealing with a narcissist who knows no boundaries in his demands, make space for yourself by saying "no" in a kind manner in moments of calm. Issuing ultimatums and blame may be a relief in the moment, but it will ultimately put you in a hard position.

Your loved one, friend, or coworker may always be a narcissist, but there are ways to heal—even if it's just within yourself. Once you understand the root of his or her behavior, you can begin to act upon it in a healthy, calm way and create a better environment for everyone. I urge you to use this book as you travel the path toward healing.

Chapter 1 - Definition of Narcissism

Personality traits vary from one person to another. However, some features that people portray are not personality traits but personality disorders. A narcissist is a person with a personality disorder called Narcissistic Personality Disorder or NPD. They are commonly termed as arrogant, self-centered, manipulative, and boastful. A person with NPD has a need for exercise attention, admiration, approval, and lacks empathy for others. They are always unwilling to recognize the needs of others. These people are generally unhappy if not given the favors and attention they want. They have trouble handling anything they perceive as critics and insist on having the best of everything.

Generally, persons with NPD portray an arrogant and haughty behavior that is boastful and pretentious. They cause problems in many areas of life, including the workplace, school, relationships, home, social, and religious groups, among others. Have problems regulating emotions and behaviors. Dealing with stress and adapting to change is almost impossible for them. The divorce from the consequences of their judgment and actions whenever these do not affect them directly. Behind the mask of their extreme confidence lies a fragile self-esteem, vulnerable to the slightest criticism. They avoid the painful realization of failure that could tarnish their perceived image. Hence, they only listen to the information they seek to hear, failing to learn from others.

Signs and Symptoms of a Narcissist

The signs and symptoms of narcissism may vary from one person to another. Some other psychological health issues like alcohol and drug addict may cause signs that overlap with those of NPD. However, some are common and distinct among people who have this personality disorder.

1. An Exaggerated Sense of Self-Importance

Narcissist portrays a grandiosity characteristic. This is more than arrogance. They possess an unrealistic sense of self-superiority. In their world of fantasy, they think they are unique, special, and way too high beyond the ordinary. They consider themselves the undisputed star and expect everyone to find their importance.

In this trait, narcissists think themselves in the center of the universe. They believe that they are too crucial that everything has to revolve around them. Even when they have done nothing to deserve it, they expect other people to adore them always

2. Seek Much Attention and Entitlement

Occasional compliments are never enough for a narcissist. They have an obsessive need for constant soothing of their ego. They seek to surround themselves with people who will meet these demands. For them is to prey on those who can cater to their affirmation, attention, and entitlement.

Being in a union with such a person can be toxic. They never care about the well beings of other people. With a narcissist, it is not about to give and take; it is present, give, and endless giving. With that, you can quickly lose your self-worth other life goals to cater for the full attention the narcissist wants.

3. Expect recognition as superior even without warranting achievements.

Magical thinking and self-deception are some of the significant characteristics of a person with NPD. They live in a fantasy world full of distortion. Their exaggerated self-image helps them avoid the deep feeling of insecurity. Even when they know, they deserve criticism, the demand for unique affirmation without minding how others will take it.

These kinds of people cannot cope with any failure. If you try to point at their mistakes, they respond with a vigorous defense. They become cold and aggressive towards anyone who wants to criticize them. All they believe is that they are perfect, and they expect excellent superior recognition no matter how terrible they are.

A feeling of threat from a confident and famous person is shared among the narcissist. Whenever they encounter a person who tends to point out their puffed up idealized self, contempt becomes their defense mechanism. They neutralize the threat and do it in a dismissive and chaotic way. In this, they demonstrate how little, and less significant others are.

Toxic narcissist conduct smear campaigns against someone they may want to bring down. They even spread false information. Stalking is also typical to them. They invade other people's boundaries and invade their privacy. In this, they try to find evidence and prove how horrible the other party is. They sabotage reputation, influence everyone against you, and mistreat you. After they make sure that you have no one to fall back to, they feel safe to finish your psyche impairment. They show you how little you are and how much they have the right to look down upon you.

4. Take Advantage of Others

To a narcissist, other people are taken as objects to be used to achieve their unrealistic needs. They cannot put themselves in other people's shoes and identify with their feelings. They have no sense of empathy. Their interpersonal relationships are one-sided, malicious, and exploiting. They don't consider how their behavior affects others, and even if they are told, they can't get it.

A narcissist knows not what genuine compassion is. They are capable of laughing at your most painful tears. They do horrible things to a person and feel no sense of guilt.

A narcissist rarely offers anything for free, even a definite compliment. Most of them act helpful and kind; that is a bait to lure you. They sugar coat their malicious endeavors to get you to seal the deal. In this deal, you will be the loser and they the gainer.

5. Monopolized Conversations

Narcissists have no room for listening and not recognizing other people's needs. To them, what they want you to say is what is important to them. Other people's opinions are met with resistance band contempt, especially if it does not fit within their magical lane.

If you start a conversation with a narcissist, the chances are that it shall be redirected. If it is about something like a positive achievement, they redirect it towards themselves. They start showing how much they contributed to it. They end up taking all the glory, even when they made zero contribution to the matter at hand. If it is about something negative like an appropriate behavior, it is redirected toward you. They make you carry all the blame. They can even pull out your past similar mistake to show you how bad you are.

6. Easily Provoked by a Slight Criticism

The narcissist is those people who it is said that you don't dare to mess up with. Anybody who gets to their wrong side has to pay. They cannot forgive any form of disrespect. They demand respect and adoration, and of course, they pay it back with disdain.

If you try to be aggressive to a narcissist, they take it differently. To them, they find it an excellent chance to find evidence to use against you. At this point, they play victim, show how bad you mistreat them, and add salt to it. A malicious narcissist can even provoke you intentionally so that you react, and they find a chance to fulfill their mission.

7. Preoccupied with fantasies about success, power, and perfection

Narcissists are full of an inflated self-image. Even their conversations are full of brag on how important they are, how perfect their life is, and how lucky other peoples are to have them in their lives. A total irony!

With this trait, they believe that they are of a higher class. They associate with people that they perceive as high class. They never care about the personality of a person. To them, all that matters is a person's title, the house they live, the car they drive, and other material things.

In their fantasy, they become envious of anybody who threatens to compete with their 'untouchable' selves. They also believe that other people will envy their 'good' lives. This makes them live in imagined insecurity.

Narcissism is chronic. It has a long-term pattern of abnormal behavior. Medical treatment can help in this condition, but it cannot be cured. The state requires medical diagnosis and not laboratory tests or imaginations.

Nevertheless, due to their perfection mentality, narcissistic people may refuse medical attention, bearing in mind that they never want to accept that anything is wrong with them. Whenever they may find themselves in the hands of medical personnel, it is more likely to be due to signs of depression, drug abuse, or another mental health problem. Chances of them not wanting to go through the treatment are high. Thus close monitoring is required in this case.

Where Narcissist Stem From

According to the article Narcissistic Personally Disorder (NPD), NPD affects 1% of the population. Although most individuals have the traits, most manifest in a pathological form as NPD, where the individual overestimates his/her ability and excess need for admiration.

The Making of a Narcissist

Narcissist personality is generally misunderstood by the public. It tends to be associated with having an inflated ego. The out-word sign of narcissism is the constant crave for superiority and pursuit of it.

A narcissist has projected trust issues. They do not trust anyone in any relationship. For these reasons, they alert and ready to fight back so as not to subdue. Despite their enforced superiority, narcissists have a deep feeling of anxiety and hypervigilance. They experience hallucinations like fear of unknown reasons that could make them vulnerable.

Chapter 2 - Causes of Narcissistic Personality Disorder

When looking at the statistics, the figure of approximately one percent of the population having narcissistic personality disorder seems eerily high—uncomfortably high, perhaps. By now, we've built up a broader and stronger idea of who is normally affected by it. As we can see, narcissistic personality disorder certainly doesn't discriminate, though there is a number of criteria that make somebody more likely to have the disorder, and it does seem to occur more commonly in men than in women.

Despite looking at the people that narcissistic personality disorder occurs within—or, rather, the groups which seem to present with his disorder the most—we still haven't looked at a huge number of the root causes

The exact causes of narcissistic personality disorder are currently unknown. There are a number of indirect suppositions as to what causes it, and all of these culminate into what is the general modern vision of what leads to the development of this disorder.

The going consensus on what leads to the development of narcissistic personality disorder is that it's ultimately a combination of genetic, social, environmental, and biological factors. The exact role that each of these plays in the development of this disorder can vary depending upon the individual and the exact subtype of the disorder developed can vary equally as much. That is to say, there is no sure cocktail of causes that will lead to the development of one specific subtype or another.

In order to dive into the big question of "why does this happen?" a bit more, we're going to be looking at this one-by-one in order to come to a firmer understanding on what causes narcissistic personality disorder.

Firstly, let's look at the genetic aspect: there is a lot of evidence that the disorder itself can be inherited. The existence of a family member with the disorder makes it far more likely that a given individual will develop the disorder themselves. Studies performed on twins have been rather conducive to showing that there is an inheritable aspect to the disorder.

It can be difficult, though, to determine how much of this is because of the person growing up with somebody who has the disorder—for example, if somebody's father were to have narcissistic personality disorder. This no doubt would lead to the child taking in that influence and being, to one extent or another, impacted by the disorder and more likely to develop it themselves. In this case, narcissistic personality disorder could be seen as both a genetic and a social disorder.

Beyond the genetic factors, there are a number of different environmental factors at play as well. Here, we're going to be looking at both the social and environmental catalysts to the development of narcissistic personality disorder. These are largely thought to play the biggest part in the development of the disorder—larger than either the genetic or biological causes, though with environment and biology likely playing equal parts or with environment only slightly weighted in favor compared to biology.

One of the largest catalysts for the development of narcissistic personality disorder is when a child learns manipulative behavior from either their parents or their friends. Manipulative parents are extremely common, and unfortunately, manipulative parenting styles weren't condemned for a rather long time. With developmental psychology and emotional abuse only becoming topics that were largely discoursed in the second half of the 20th century, what results is the fact that there are still some rather ancient parenting styles that are incredibly unhealthy. More than that, it doesn't just come down to the parenting style; it also comes down to a person's general way of life. It's unfortunate, but due to the way that manipulative behavior works, it's possible for a manipulative person to surround themselves with people they can manipulate and never have to change their behavior. Because of this, they could teach this to a child as the norm.

With attitudes on parenting largely shifting in the twenty-first century, this problem will hopefully become less and less prominent as people start to talk about things such as mental and emotional abuse more and they become more acceptable topics of discourse. Until then, this will remain a rather prominent catalyst.

This goes hand-in-hand with another catalyst for the development of narcissistic personality disorder: emotional abuse in childhood. Manipulative behavior and emotional abuse aren't necessarily one and the same, but they do often go hand-in-hand. In the latter case, one may develop narcissistic personality disorder as a defense mechanism or coping mechanism. These can be some of the hardest cases to deal with from a psychological perspective because dealing with them means dealing with a much deeper trauma. This is compared to just trying to make people rationalize their position in other individuals who didn't have to endure emotional abuse as a child.

That isn't to say, though, that a narcissist may necessarily have developed this as a defense or coping mechanism. In fact, many people develop the disorder as a result of things which happen to them in other ways. For example, a lot of people like to take the post that there's no such thing as excessive praise for a child. However, when a child is developing, many of the actions which occur to them—if they stick out in any way—will be intensely formative and cemented into their brain forever unless they make a very active attempt to unlearn them.

If somebody is excessively praised, they may develop the idea that they're unable to do any wrong. This happens often with single parents who don't wish to lose the respect or adoration of their child, unfortunately, and I've seen it pop up in quite a few cases of such. Likewise, if a child is excessively criticized, they may develop narcissistic personality disorder as a defense mechanism.

If people tell somebody all the time that they're exceptionally beautiful or talented with little basis in reality or little realistic, earthbound feedback in response to the praise, they're at risk for the development of narcissistic personality disorder. If people overvalue somebody or indulge them too often, that person becomes far more likely to develop the disorder.

In essence, the mind desires some sort of equilibrium in terms of its interactions with other people. It does whatever it can to reach out for this equilibrium and seek it out. Believe it or not, not all minds are equally resilient and able to so handily endure some of the stresses or excesses of life. In other words, a lot of what causes narcissistic personality disorder can be seen as over-parenting. Someone who excessively gives praise, criticism, or manipulates their child puts their child at risk for the development of narcissistic personality disorder.

Parents who are narcissists themselves will often use their children as a means of self-validation and force their narcissistic behaviors onto their children. This lead, generally, to either resentment or the development of Stockholm syndrome. In the former case, people may drop contact with their parents or limit contact as much as possible. In the latter, they will often model themselves after their parents.

In terms of biological factors which correspond to the development of this disorder, there isn't a whole lot of research to work with. As I said earlier, finding finite study opportunities for narcissistic personality disorder can be difficult. However, what studies have been done have shown that the areas of the brain having to do with empathy, emotion, and compassion generally are not nearly as large as they are in neurotypical people or people without mental disorders.

One question many people might ask while reading this is whether or not they can tell if their child is a narcissist.

The thing is that while one of the things linked to the development of narcissistic personality disorder is being overly sensitive as an infant, this is one of the only signs that one has for the development of narcissistic personality disorder until adolescence is reached. There are also a number of oversensitive children that don't grow up to have this disorder. This means that in terms of a concrete answer, we're a little bit at a loss.

If there are other people who show signs of narcissistic personality disorder, or if you tend to excessively praise your child without realistic feedback or excessively criticize them, then you may have a narcissist on your hands. However, many children and teens will show the symptoms of narcissism as a passing phase before finally growing out of it. Their brains are maturing, and they have a lot to learn about the world. Depending on how young they are, just address the manner in a reasonable way relative to their age. If you're seriously concerned or your child shows an excessive amount of the symptoms, it may not be a bad idea to set up a trip to a child psychiatrist in order to have them professionally evaluated. If they are found to have narcissism or any related psychiatric disorder, your psychiatrist will work with you and your child in order to chart a path forward.

Chapter 3 - Healthy and Extreme Narcissism

Healthy Narcissism

Confidence, charisma or appreciation of your actual talents/attributes without these attributes leading you to believing you are a superior person to others, are all positive traits, encouraged by most societies. An ability to lead and inspire are similarly positive traits. These traits can be described as healthy narcissism.

Many confident, out-going, successful people have high levels of healthy narcissism and self-enhancement, believing in themselves and putting themselves forward rather than shrinking in the face of challenges and attention. But these positive aspirational mindsets lack the belief that they are "better" than anyone else, or the will to act in a superior manner. Confidence and self-belief are healthy, but over confidence and believing your positive attributes make you better than other people, crosses from healthy to extreme narcissism. Confidence and self-belief do not make healthy narcissists un-empathic or manipulative. These healthy traits should not be confused with unhealthy or damaging narcissistic traits, as often seems to be the case in many online materials.

This lines up well with Dr Malkin's finding that 1% of people score very highly on healthy narcissism, and very low on extreme narcissism-individuals who light up the room and inspire others rather than undermining them. They view both themselves and others through a rose-tinted, optimistic lens, and encourage and inspire others rather than feeling threatened by their success.

Extreme Narcissism

Narcissistic Supply, Attention and Superiority

Positive feedback, attention and approval as rewards for doing well or being a certain way are enjoyed by everyone to a degree, but those who score highly for narcissism (both healthy and extreme) increasingly revel in it. People with extreme narcissism start to need it to maintain their sense of wellbeing- protecting themselves from coming down from their high, like an alcoholic will avoid being sober. Some also have a wavering sense of self-esteem dating back prior to the development of the dependency.

For everyone, love and praise create pleasurable feelings as they release dopamine- the brain's reward neurotransmitter. For people with underlying low self-esteem, as well as those that have problems regulating their dopamine levels, this experience can be particularly attractive. The pleasurable rush acts as a "tonic" to soothe underlying feelings of pain from feeling negatively about themselves.

Dopamine is also released when an individual discovers that they have a talent and can be successful in some way, or when they discover an activity or attribute that brings them praise or positive attention (such as being attractive, being good at sport, being academically talented or achieving goals at work). For most people, this results in the pursuit and development of skills and interests and is how healthy narcissism develops. Many truly confident and kind people become attracted to attention and limelight, reveling in performing for others- think comedians or talk show hosts such as Ellen DeGeneres or James Corden. These people are probably not hiding extreme narcissism; they're likely to just be friendly, outgoing and confident.

This can result in rapid cycling of moods, and a constant seeking out of more supply to maintain the high. Side effects of plummeting dopamine levels include feelings of depression, anxiety and irritability. These cycling moods do nothing for the extreme narcissist's sense of self-esteem, particularly if low self-esteem pre-existed before the dependency. Feelings of guilt and shame may then exacerbate the cycle-propelling the extreme narcissist to remain inflated and enter a state of denial about what it is like to be around them when they crash, and how they then interact with the world.

Those who score highly for extreme narcissism can become competitive for the limited "supply" that they receive from those around them. If we imagine the attention of one individual as a small package of "drugs," we can see how this works. The amount of drug is limited, and the addict wants much of it for themselves. Extreme narcissistic people are frequently threatened and jealous of those around them, reacting viciously to maintain their supply and their sense of "goodness," "correctness" or superiority. They may use many forms of manipulation to get as much narcissistic supply as they can, whilst justifying it to themselves.

Experiences that cause the release of dopamine- such as drinking alcohol, taking drugs, having sex, or smoking cigarettes- are known to be potentially addictive for this reason. The pleasurable release of dopamine and inflated self-esteem from narcissistic supply, offers an escape from naturally low dopamine levels, or the pain of feeling as though the narcissist is defective or "bad" in some way.

At higher points along the spectrum, the constant need for validation and praise can reach unquenchable levels, where no amount of "supply" is enough to maintain the narcissist's inflated sense of self.

Perceived criticism or mistakes made by a vulnerable narcissist can result in an almost instantaneous and crippling return to this state of low self-esteem. However, when under threat our cognitive defenses may be extremely adept at protecting us from experiencing this type of pain.

Narcissistic defense responses may kick in to block out the threat and "save" the narcissist from facing what, to others, would constitute taking responsibility for their actions. To those that are lower on the narcissistic scale, this shows up as the more narcissistic party becoming defensive and refusing to take responsibility for their hurtful words and actions. They may attack in response to any perceived insult or threat to their self-esteem. To the individual at hand, however, this choice between taking responsibility and remaining defensive may well be the difference between staying afloat and functional and breaking down completely.

Can Extreme Narcissists Love?

The claim that narcissistic people "cannot love" is an over-simplified and negative view that does not look at the technicalities of what is happening between narcissistic highs and defenses. This idea forgets the nuances and complications of human beings. Claiming that all narcissistic mothers are not able to love their children, or that a narcissistic spouse is not able to love their partner is black and white, unrealistic thinking.

So, what's going on? People who have extreme narcissism traits are frequently inflating themselves to feel good, defending themselves against "crashes," and protecting their egos against injury, meaning they may think of themselves a great deal, without much time to think of others.

Whether people who demonstrate a high frequency of extreme narcissistic tendencies can feel love in the typical sense, is likely to depend on the individual. They can certainly undergo the same "infatuation" response as the rest of us, releasing and becoming "hooked" on dopamine and feeling as though they are falling in love. Ironically, being in love may feel like a beautiful experience involving a cherished and idolized partner, but it has been shown to be inherently selfish. People that are in love seek to serve their own emotional needs, rather than predominantly empathizing with their partners' (those on the receiving end of unrequited love have been shown to be more capable of empathizing with the "in love" party, than the person who is in love is able to empathize with them).

Whether feelings of being in love from the extreme narcissists' point of view resemble healthier individual's experiences is open to talk about. Whether these feelings progress further to feelings of romantic love, and then on to a sense of attachment that is comparable to healthier individuals are also not conclusive and is also likely to vary from person to person.

Most narcissistic people – lower down the scale, who spend much of their time "untriggered" – may be perfectly capable of feeling love and empathy during those times. Extreme narcissistic people may, however, fear falling in love because they may view themselves as unworthy or incapable. This can cause them to dread the pain and vulnerability love would bring when their partner eventually left or betrayed them.

However, just because they fear it, deny it, or have little time to dedicate to it, does not mean that they are invulnerable to it. They may not be able to express it in healthy ways. If a feeling of vulnerability from falling in love is anxiety-provoking, they may seek to assuage this feeling by indulging in infidelity, belittling their partner, forming multiple attachments to lower the strength of the primary attachment, or attempt to lower the value of their partner in some way.

Love and compassion for others cannot take priority at times when narcissistic reactions are taking place. The chance to gain supply or the need to defend against a threat to the ego must first diminish before loving feelings can emerge or be expressed. In cases where these activities are a full-time pursuit, love and empathy may never happen.

Defense against emotional pain, sits very high on the brain's automatic priorities list. Love sits lower in the brain's list of automated priorities. Which doesn't mean that love is valued less by our logical brains or value systems. It means that our brains' automated responses (which are subconscious and unconscious) move first to protect us from emotional pain, before considering higher notions such as love and empathy.

Chapter 4 - Types of Narcissists

It's not easy to try and work out why some people are narcissists and others aren't. Of course, we know that Narcissistic Personality Disorder is a condition, but there are countless other theories, which swirl around the same subject. For instance, Freud put forth the idea that all children go through a stage of development which includes something called "primary narcissism". It is at this point in their lives that they haven't yet grasped the idea that people are separate, need to be respected, etc. However, as normal development continues, this idea disappears, and the healthy ideas of an adult take over.

In addition, a lot of research has gone into different types of narcissists. It's important to know the main differences so you can learn more about the subject in general. This will help you in your situation because you'll have more solid information on which to base your final decision.

If you break it down, there are actually two main types of narcissists - vulnerable narcissists and grandiose narcissists, who are also sometimes referred to as invulnerable narcissists.

Vulnerable narcissists are hard to spot because they don't come over as overly confident and if anything, they can seem shy. However, underneath it all, it can be quite a different story.

Vulnerable narcissists often have deep-seated feelings of loathing and in order to cover those up, they tend to create an illusion or impression of themselves which deflects how they really feel. They connect with those in power or those they assume to be more popular and they have no problem in stamping over anyone to be connected.

As with most types of narcissists, vulnerable narcissists don't care about the feelings of other people and have a total lack of empathy. One of the key tactics this type of narcissist uses is emotional manipulation, with gaslighting being the most common route. This helps to get the "you poor thing" type of sympathy they need to feel better about themselves and deal with their low self-worth.

On the other hand, the grandiose narcissist or invulnerable narcissist is the most common type and the one that you will associate the most with the picture of a narcissist. This person thinks they're better than everyone else, dresses to impress and doesn't care who they hurt. They're very confident, and don't display the same low self-worth that a vulnerable narcissist does. If anything they have a very thick skin!

Within these two main types however, it's these subtypes which allow you to really pinpoint the type of narcissist you're dealing with.

Amorous Narcissism

This type of narcissist focuses on attracting as many people as possible, usually has many one-night stands, and doesn't care who knows about it.

Their level of self-worth is reflected in the number of people they sleep with and they're usually extremely charming, to get people to fall under their spell. You'll often hear of amorous narcissists being referred to as 'heartbreakers', because not only are they extremely charming and usually very well dressed/well turned out, but they don't care who they hurt in the end.

Compensatory Narcissism

This type of narcissist is trying to cover up or forget something which has happened to them in the past, possibly in their childhood. They'll usually create an image that is a total fantasy and they may appear completely overconfident. This type of narcissist is likely to prey on those who are shy or emotionally weaker and is usually quite drawn to empaths too. Emotional manipulation is very commonly used by a compensatory empath.

Elitist Narcissism

This type of narcissist has to be the very best of everything, they have to have everything, and they have to be the most well-known. They will tread on anyone in order to get where they want to be, and they do not care who they hurt along the way. They are usually associated with others who are high up in their profession, simply because they've identified them and made sure that they become connected.

Malignant Narcissism

This type of narcissist is without a doubt the most dangerous to be around and if you do come into contact with this type of person, you need to get out of the situation as quickly as possible. This narcissist is dangerous, hurtful and very damaging and can often share the same traits as a sociopath or psychopath. This narcissist has zero care for feelings and doesn't understand morals. They have no care for remorse and they sometimes even feel delighted at the hurt they cause. Malignant narcissists are often in trouble with the law, more often than not.

As we begin to learn more about narcissism in general, there are sure to be more labels placed on different types. For now, however, we know the basic traits that make up a narcissist person, regardless of the type that you want to call them. Can you identify your partner in this list?

Chapter 5 - Treatments for Narcissistic Personality Disorder

Although there are treatments for people with NPD, this can be a very difficult disorder to eradicate. Most therapists find that helping the patient manage the symptoms is the best course of treatment for people with NPD. There are several reasons this disorder can be difficult to deal with in a therapeutic setting.

First, these traits are so ingrained into the person's psyche, it is quite hard to change them. This is primarily because behavior started forming at a very young age, when most personality traits develop in childhood. Second, the nature of NPD can make it extremely difficult to treat. People who suffer from this disorder believe themselves to be smarter than others around them, more capable, and deserving of special treatment. This means that they don't usually recognize that there is a problem at all. Usually, only a concerted effort by the people in their lives to point out their issues will bring someone to therapy. Of course, for therapy to be successful, the patient must admit that there is a problem. Also, once they are in therapy, the patients tend to devalue the therapist, making it difficult to form the therapeutic bond between patient and therapist that can help the patient relate to the therapist, which allows them to explore their disorder.

Many psychiatrists and psychologists have difficulty treating someone with NPD because they often have a blatant disregard for their doctors or therapists, believing that they know more about what is wrong than the therapists. They may even try to intimidate their caregivers to prevent them from helping the patient change.

Even with these difficulties in treatment, there are options available for those with NPD. These are listed below:

Individual Therapy

In individual therapy, a therapist works with the patient on a one-on-one basis. The goal of therapy is to help the patient form better relationships with others, to help them understand that others are separate people from the NPD sufferer, with their own goals, ideas, and needs, and to get to the root cause of the narcissistic behaviors that led to the problem in the first place. This is generally not a short-term prospective, and someone with NPD could spend years in therapy to achieve all these goals. However, that is no reason to get discouraged. Some changes can take place very quickly if the patient is interested in change and is willing to do some work. The changes can result from the patient being willing to monitor their behavior and modify it when it is unacceptable.

For example, teaching the patient to understand their feelings and to regulate them can be taken cared of pretty quickly with Cognitive-Behavioral Therapy. Working with a patient to get them to understand a different viewpoint from their own can also be a first step in a therapy session. The patient can be taught to differentiate their own thoughts, feelings, and ideas, from others and can learn to identify when they are overstepping their boundaries.

Other things that can be covered in therapy includes helping the patient deal with criticism and failure. Since a person suffering from NPD believes they are above reprisal, being offered criticism or having something not work out for them can become a very difficult situation where they lash out at those around them or blame the failure on others. A therapist can help this person learn to recognize their mistakes, encourage them to stop deflecting blame, and what to do when faced with a situation of failure or criticism. The patient will learn that there are better ways to deal with criticism than acting out.

Another area of change that can be dealt with in therapy is to help someone with NPD learn to see and understand the feelings of other people around them including:

- Teaching the patient to become more conscious of their actual abilities and limits. Therapists can help the patient accurately identify their strengths and weaknesses, when they need help, and where their limits lie.
- Teaching them to accept constructive criticism.
- Help the patient deal with self-esteem issues. After all, many people with NPD may have an inflated sense of self that shows to the outside world, but deep inside, they may be utilizing an inflated sense of self to cover up what is really a low self-esteem.
- After trust has been developed in the therapeutic relationship, the therapist can begin to delve into the underlying causes of the

person's narcissism, such as childhood trauma. This is the part of therapy that will take the most time and energy.

Group Therapy

Working with a therapist in a group setting is also a great idea for someone with narcissistic personality disorder. This gives the person the opportunity to interact with others, in a controlled setting, to teach them how to interact effectively. When a person suffering from NPD engages in group therapy, they can learn self-control when dealing with others, have other patients like them point out when they are being unreasonable, and act out confrontations with a therapist trained in dealing with this disorder. By doing so, the patient can learn better functioning with others. It also enables the patient to learn to identify others as separate from themselves, under the guidance of other patients who are further along in the process and a trained therapist. This can help to accelerate the learning process for the person with NPD. Also, patients further along in the therapeutic process can help newer patients. Individuals can learn a great deal from each other, when given the opportunity.

Medication

Although there are many psychiatric medications available on the market, most do not directly treat the symptoms of NPD. Instead, medications can be prescribed to deal with indirect issues that a person with NPD may have, such as anxiety (especially when going through therapy for low-self-esteem issues) and depression. Many psychiatrists feel that psychotropic medications are not helpful in any way to someone suffering from NPD.

Hospitalization

In extreme cases, someone with severe NPD may be hospitalized in a psychiatric facility. This could happen when a person's symptoms are so severe that they become a danger to themselves or others. Because of the volatility of people with NPD, it is possible that they could place themselves in danger because they have difficulty telling what a real danger is and may take behaviors to the extreme. Their lack of impulse control could contribute to dangerous behaviors. Also, if someone upsets them, it is possible that they could take their aggressions out against someone else. Again, their inability to control their impulses may lead them to physically lash out at others.

It is recommended that any hospitalization for NPD be short term and should be concentrated on dealing with the specific symptom that brought them to the hospital in the first place. Long-term hospitalization has not been shown to be effective for people with NPD.

The most effective treatment for NPD is psychotherapy, both individual and group therapy. Used in conjunction, these therapies can be used to help the sufferer of Narcissistic Personality Disorder develop more stable relationships and develop a more realistic self-view. They can learn to manage and modify their behavior. They can also be taught to understand the underlying causes of their behavior, which may help them to deal more effectively with their issues.

Chapter 6 - How to Escape from Narcissist's Manipulation

The narcissist intends to win. There is no mutuality and consideration. One essential advice is to limit your exposure to the narcissist. Do not talk to her if you are stressed, tired, or irritable. Your goal is to stay calm and do your best not to expose your emotional triggers. Take a deep breath and reconnect with your body. We often remember how cruel these confrontations can get and may feel anxiety just thinking about her or how even hearing her voice may trigger panic. You need to be grounded and be as clear as you can by not reacting from memories of the past. You know already that the narcissist won't change, but you can, and you will. It is imperative also to understand that conversations can get highly charged and emotional, so don't be shocked or surprised when the narcissist brings up delicate subject matters. She is not capable of empathy, consideration, or sincerity. Therefore, don't expect that from her. It is important so that you can establish healthy boundaries.

When you are dealing with a controlling person, it may be essential to adjust your expectations and realize that setting boundaries is a continuous process. She may act like she does not hear you; therefore, be prepared to repeat yourself. But also know your limit because the narcissist will test you to see whether you will soften your boundaries and will make allowances. She will test to see how far she can push you.

Also, be prepared that when you start setting boundaries with the narcissist, her attacks and tantrums may escalate. She is not used to hearing the word "no."

Since you are dealing with a pathological mind, you can't use healthy logic because the narcissist's brain does not work like ours. If you think that you are going to get the narcissist to feel pain like they've inflicted on you, you're wrong. They rewrite the whole story and make up a new reality as to what happened. And they often get people around them to believe that, as well because they are so good at lying.

Here are some ways that you can take control of the interactions you have with narcissists.

1. Work on your internal healing. If you've come from a dysfunctional family or you've spent a long time with a narcissist, you have emotional wounds that have been caused by the narcissist, and it makes you act in specific ways that make you a target for a narcissist. When you deal with those wounds, and you heal them, you no longer operate for the narcissist, and you can have a much more happy and successful life. Being brought up in a dysfunctional environment, you might be a people pleaser, you are disassociated from your authentic self, and you most probably have very low self-esteem; so those are the things that you need to work on. When you work on that, you stop having triggers that the narcissist can affect you with.

2. Don't give them any positive or negative emotions at all. Having conversations with narcissists, they usually say something that hurts you. What they're expecting you to do is to feel hurt and then become angry towards them, so they are transferring anger onto you, and you're projecting it out, and then they feel good; they get a cathartic release.

8. So, what you can do is whatever she says to you, you need to reply in a calm and collected voice, "you seem angry," and the narcissist will say, "No, I'm not angry!" and she will carry on. Then you must clip the conversation, carry on in a neutral tone, or don't talk to her at all. Carry on with what you were doing, but don't give her any positive or negative emotions at all. In this way, you're starving her of narcissistic supply she was expecting.

3. If narcissists shame you, agree with them. They don't know what to say. But be careful with something like this if you are going through a divorce because the narcissist might be recording you and what you say might be taken out of text in a court of law. So, you obviously must be careful about where you're using that, but it's a very effective and powerful technique for stopping a narcissist from making you feel bad. You are repeating back to them everything they're saying to you so that they can see the ridiculousness of their statements.

4. Be very careful about showing your cards. If the narcissist attacks you, the more you try to explain that you didn't do anything wrong, the weaker your position is going to become. You have to keep quiet. That's a way of holding your strengths, and it will help you with outsmarting a narcissist.

5. If the narcissist is constantly criticizing you, close your mouth, so you don't agree or disagree with her, carry on with whatever you are doing. That will infuriate them because they were trying to make you feel bad, and that's their way of getting narcissistic supply. Narcissists are like emotional vampires; they live on other people's emotions, whether they be positive or negative.

6. If she tries to point out your faults to get her narcissistic supply out of you, then flip the mirror on her and point out her faults. Whatever she is saying to you, realize that is the weak point, and if you turn the mirror on her, then she goes into a narcissistic rage, and you are going to stop her from trying to drain you psychologically.

7. Be careful if narcissists are nice to you; there's always a reason, so don't fall into their trap.

8. You must remain very calm, also when dealing with other people. Whether she is going to take your children or whether she has turned everybody on you, if you show your emotions you will fall into her trap, and she will also twist it so that you look guilty. There's a good chance she started hinting to people that there's something wrong with you emotionally or psychologically, and if you freak out then people think the narcissist was right.

9. Don't speak badly about the narcissist with people who knows her. If you want to tell them something that the narcissist has done, at first you have to say how much you like the narcissist, and you are so upset that it hasn't worked out or something like that depending on your situation. Sometimes narcissists get all their friends and all your extended family against you, so you

have to tell them first of all how much you love them and how much you are upset that there's a problem. Then you have got to mention something that they do and how you admire them for that, and so then you can tell them the bad things that they've done, that have affected you and then after that you should make like a weak excuse as to why they did that "oh well, I don't know, maybe it's just the personality, or they had a hard upbringing."

In this way, you are first showing that you're a loving person and that you see good things in them. It's showing that even though they've done these horrible things, you can still try and make some excuse for them. Such it puts you in a much better light. Narcissists used this kind of thing for years behind your back, saying how much they love you and care about you but hinting at things that were wrong with you.

10. If the narcissist tries to say that there's something wrong with you, don't try to explain, be cheerful, carry on with what you're doing. For example, if she says to you "why are you so depressed?" or "why are you so angry?" or whatever you are or not, you need to say "no, I'm not" and then remain calm.

These techniques help you to stop feeding the narcissist and stay in control of the situation. You should not stay in a long-term relationship with a narcissist, but these techniques are useful to control the situation when you are dealing with her.

Chapter 7 - Setting Boundaries From a Narcissist

Everyone needs boundaries but narcissists more than most because they are essentially still children inside. Therefore, when communicating with them it useful to think about how you would communicate with an infant rather than the adult they present as.

No/Low Contact

Limit your contact with them as much as is humanly possible. If you have children use a mediator or communication app. This reinforces that their behavior is not acceptable, and they will get no attention from you when they "misbehave".

Easier said than done right!? Especially when you have children. But here are some practical ways you can do this.

No Contact

No contact doesn't just mean not texting them or taking their calls. It means deleting their number, blocking them on social media and not asking your friends and family about them. You literally don't want any contact with them. This is by far the easiest way to move on because you have the space to heal. The quote "you can't heal in the same environment you got sick" is true. You need freedom from them and their mind games. If you give them the slightest morsel or contact, they will begin with the tactics of hoovering and love-bombing to get you embroiled once more in their drama. And you will set yourself back. Obviously if you have done this already or do find yourself back in it, that's OK. Relapse is somewhat inevitable as narcissistic abuse is like a heroin addiction. You want to feel the relief that they are offering. But remember it is short term relief. They are a drug and drugs are BAD!

My advice is to recruit a friend to act as your willpower. When you feel yourself tempted, reach out to your friend instead and they will bolster you to resist temptation.

Warning though, it will hurt. You will grieve. You won't understand why because your logical brain knows it is exactly the right thing to do but your emotional brain is craving the attachment. Allow yourself time to go through the stages of grief - anger, denial. bargaining, depression and finally acceptance. FYI the bargaining stage will be where you are most vulnerable to contacting them or snooping on their social media. Be aware of this and prepare yourself.

Also be aware that going no-contact triggers a deep trauma within the narcissist and so this will be the most active and dangerous time. They will try:

- Hoovering - narcissists hate to lose supply and so they will attempt to lure you back in. It will start innocently enough with some form of contact. Maybe a "can I collect my stuff?" or "my friend told me you weren't at work, just wanted to check you are ok". It's bait to see if you are serious about no contact. If you are, you will probably skip ahead to smear campaigns. If not, love-bombing comes next.
- Love-bombing - They will lavish you with loving messages, gifts, promises of how they realize the error of their ways and you are the only person they love. It will be like music to your ears after the pain of separation and it will absolutely trigger your own abandonment wounds. But it is the same lies they told you in the relationship, no-one can change in a few days or a week or even a month. Especially when it is a lifetime of behaviors. I know you want to believe them, but the reality is NPD requires years of specialized therapy to address the disorder. If they really have been through that the likelihood is that they won't contact, you because they understand now how much they hurt you and would never want to re-open that wound for you. So, if they are back, they still lack empathy and simply do not care about the pain they caused.
- Smear campaign - you have resisted them so far and now they experience narcissistic injury. You have wronged them so badly that they have to punish you

and they will use every means possible. Children. Friends. Family. Professionals. Pets. They will triangulate everyone into the drama and paint you as the abuser. In fact, they will use your firm "no contact" rule as "evidence" of how abusive you are being - "they won't even talk to me to tell me what happened". This is designed to weaken your resolve and make contact as well as giving them a clear narrative that they aren't the problem, you are. Nothing you do or say to any of the flying monkeys will change the story. The absolute best thing you can do here is to remain "no contact" and ride it out. Give them nothing. A strong sense of self is needed here and if this is something you struggle with; I highly recommend getting professional help from an experienced therapist.

- When you step out of the abuser, victim and enabler triangle, the narcissist has no choice but to find someone else to fill the spot you left open. They may use your children, so it is important to help build their resilience to withstand the pressure.

- Low Contact

- If you have children, you will struggle to go no contact but there are ways for you to give yourself the space to heal whilst maintaining open communication about the children. Or the narcissist may be a family member who you aren't ready/willing to cut out of your life completely but recognize you need to limit your contact with them.

- Set up a clear strategy for dealing with "emergencies" including what constitutes an emergency
- You know the narcissist will do anything and everything to trample all over your boundaries and using the children is easy pickings for them. They will go against your requests but use the "it's about the children" or "it's an emergency" to lure you into breaching your own boundaries. This just provides them with the confirmation that they are powerful and in charge.
- Emergencies could include:
    - Health issues
    - Unable to collect/return child(ren)
    - Urgent appointment
- Both of you need to agree to these but you if they are unwilling, have them as your own standard.
- Also clearly state what and how the other party will be notified about the emergency. Again, narcissists love to keep control so they will often keep you in the dark about situations or communicate through a channel never used so that they can say "I tried to notify you, it's not my fault you didn't check". Make sure it is something you can access but isn't intrusive. So, phone calls for example might be a definite "no" but a text is OK.
- State what is to happen in the case of an emergency. Things to consider:
    - Are they to be returned to the primary caregiver?
    - Does the parent they are with deal with the emergency and notify the other parent on an hourly basis?

Remember to consider your own personal boundaries whilst ensuring that the children's needs are met.

Be clear on methods and times for communication

Be clear when and how communication can take place and enforce the consequences of not adhering to this. If you have agreed calls with children with, they are in the other parent's care, set clear times when the children will be available and on what platform. This can be agreed weekly, monthly or annually depending on the lifestyle of the parents. Do not accept calls or texts outside of these times.

Equally if you have calls agreed to the children when they are in their care, do not deviate from the times agreed. Even if they don't answer. A huge part of boundary setting is you maintaining them as well because the second you breach; the narcissist will see it as evidence that they can breach too. Yes, it will be hard but think about the bigger picture and the long-term peace you will get if you stick to it.

I recommend having one main platform for communication with the children with a back-up platform just in case. So, Facetime is the preferred platform but if there is an issue with that, Skype. Nothing else unless agreed to by both parties.

Accept the losses

This is a tough one, but the reality is, you will lose people through this process and may have to implement these strategies with people other than the narcissist. Particularly flying monkeys. The work I do with clients is always on building their own self-esteem and identity. You feel the pain of this so much more acutely when you lack a secure sense of self. This may be from your own childhood where you were perhaps not validated and so sought out that love and acceptance from others. Leading you right into the path of the narcissist. The narcissist knows this wound runs deep and uses it to hurt you and destroy you. Therefore, it is so important that you heal your own trauma so that their methods have less power. I am not going to sugar coat this though. It does hurt. But you can recover and life a narcissist free life.

Chapter 8 - The Narcissistic Relationship Pattern

Not all relationships are toxic and imbalanced, and even so, a majority of relationships, even platonic or work-related ones, will develop patterns. Patterns are evident in our daily life activities: the pattern of your workday, the pattern when you come home, the routine with your spouse or partner about who cooks and who cleans after supper, or the routine or pattern of when you go to sleep and your nighttime rituals.

All patterns begin somewhere and develop or change over time, and in any relationship, you have in your life, a lot of patterns will change while many stay the same. If you tend to date men or women who have certain tendencies or attributes, in this case, NPD, then you will already be comfortable with these patterns, and perhaps, not realize that you are repeating the same patterns over and over again by being drawn to similar types of people.

Patterns are the life grooves that get worn into our consciousness and mental state. They are the basis of how we think, react, feel, and treat others and ourselves. Patterns, like bad habits, can be broken and will only require that you acknowledge what the patterns are in the first place so that you know what needs to change.

As with any relationship, typical narcissistic relationships will follow a general pattern that causes the partners involved to exist in a repetitive cycle. Otherwise, the pattern is the general rule of thumb for how the narcissist will operate in every relationship. The usual pattern has three stages, including idealizing the partner, devaluing them, and finally discarding them. It is an emotional rollercoaster, and it can repeat itself, depending on how many times you are willing to go on this ride without facing the truth of what is going on.

Let's explore the stages so that you figure out what stage you might currently be in with your partner, or if you can recognize a common theme in your relationship from these patterns.

Idealize

In the first stages of the romantic partnership, a narcissistic person will create a reality with their partner that involves a feeling of infatuation and otherworldliness, almost as if it was destiny that the two of you came together. The sensation is of true love and a beautiful and inspiring courtship coming into being. Some people have described this part of the stage as intoxicating or like being on a drug and the high lasts for weeks, months, and occasionally longer than that.

It is not abnormal to feel the love high in the beginning stages of any relationship, and it is greatly common for couples to inspire this feeling in each other as they get closer and form the love bond. In the case of the narcissistic relationship, the following stages offer a broader explanation of how it is different than other love relationships in their blossoming stage.

People who have reported being in narcissistic relationships have described the "idealize" stage like finding a soulmate and are on a cloud of beautiful life possibilities with their partner. The sensation is that you will never fall apart and that you are meant to be together. This connection is offered greatly by the narcissist who will "drug" their partner with loving words, dedications, praise, courting rituals, intense sexual relations, regular vacations or trips, promises of creating a future life together, and the admonishment of being the most important and special person they have ever met.

It sounds amazing, doesn't it? And who wouldn't want to have such a whirlwind romance right from the get-go? Isn't that what every romantic comedy is selling to you? The "love bomb" phase of the relationship feels like a dream come true, and the reality is that anyone who experienced something like this would probably have a hard time being skeptical, especially when they are being promised the world and that love will last forever.

The next stage creates the platform for understanding the true nature of the narcissistic relationship after the "honeymoon" phase has worn out their ability to gain "narcissistic supply."

Devalue

As the relationship enters a more realistic and comfortable rhythm, the intensity may not be as extreme, and some aspects of the connection may start to wane or grown faded. There are moments of disagreement and possible attempts to confront the narcissist about their attitude or behavior, with a reaction that is not what you might expect from someone who is so deeply in love with you, as they demonstrated before.

The large, red flags on the tropical paradise, love island you created together start to paint another picture of reality. It happens slowly and subtly and can sometimes even feel stealthy, cunning, and deceptive. The objective of the narcissist is to devalue their partner in covert ways to attain a level of emotional superiority, in effect, causing their partner to establish an urge or desire to rekindle the level of affection that they had experienced in the first stages of becoming acquainted with each other.

The narcissist quietly bullies while their partner, or the victim of narcissistic abuse, works tirelessly to bring the sensuality and love back into the courtship by falling for the game and asking the narcissist what they can do to change or "fix it."

In a lot of situations, a person might see these red flags and not feel attached to the narcissist, choosing instead to let the relationship naturally dissolve into the final stage (discarding). However, in many cases, the partner of the narcissist will want to remind themselves of how magical the opening of the affair was and that it must be true love, and therefore, worth seeking out solutions to whatever issues are arising.

The patterns will continue in the "devaluing" stage, as the narcissist will not want to comply with any kind of growth and will create emotional and mental (occasionally physical) abuse in the form of gaslighting, putting down their partner with verbal comments, avoiding or withdrawing emotional or physical intimacy as a form of punishment, disappearing for periods of time without word, withholding seduction or affection, and blaming their partner for anything that might be an issue with them (projecting).

This stage can continue for a while, but eventually, if the partner of the narcissist is not complying with their demands, needs, and expectations, then they will be discarded and cast off.

Discard

If the partner of the narcissist cannot provide them with adequate narcissistic supply, then they will be discarded without emotion or need for debate. If the partner asks for a kind of compromise, honesty, relationship counseling, healthy boundaries, or mutual exchange, then the narcissist will likely determine that they are no longer with the "perfect partner." What they want is someone who can always feed their ego without the demand for anything else in return, and so, if you are not able to meet these demands, you are no longer a viable partner for the narcissist.

Keep in mind, as you read this that it is totally and completely normal and healthy to ask for reciprocity, balance, comradery, communication, and compromise in your relationships. These qualities and attributes, however, are not commonly practiced by the narcissist and so you will be throwing bricks at a brick wall for no good reason if you ask them to compromise or see your side of things.

In a codependent partnership or a situation between a narcissist and an empath, the relationship can be a lifelong pattern (idealize, devalue, discard - over and over again) that will never fully reach a full discarding of the relationship. However, the act of discarding can occur as a result of not meeting the narcissist's needs, and it will be an emotional discarding and punishment that can only be rectified by the partner of the narcissist succumbing to the emotional needs and demands of the narcissist's ego.

Either way, the discarding stage can feel like a huge shock to the victim or target of narcissistic abuse, because it began with such passion, love, and admiration. How can such a loving and amiable person become so different and not even care about your special bond? The answer is that they never truly cared, and they were simply looking for someone to feed their ego and offer them narcissistic supply. If you can't meet that demand, then you're out.

Unfortunately, this can happen all of the time, especially if you don't know what patterns or flags to observe when you are getting involved with someone. It can be very hard to tell at the beginning of a relationship if someone is a narcissist, and they may be a healthy narcissist at that. The key is identifying the patterns in the devaluing stage so that you don't end up shocked, confused, and alone with a stack of insecurities and neuroses about yourself that you were convinced of having by your narcissistic partner.

The effects of this pattern over time can be exhausting and detrimental to you. If you have already engaged in this type of pattern before and you keep going through it with certain patterns, stop blaming yourself for the relationship ending after such a whirlwind start. Odds are, it's not your fault and whatever your narcissistic partner told you about yourself is not true.

Chapter 9   -   How Did You Fall for A Narcissist?

The person described above sounds horrible so this begs the question of why and how anyone would gain feelings for such an individual. There must be something wrong with people who do, right? That is incorrect.

Narcissists target their victims. They do not go after just anyone. People who are honest, compassionate, authentic, and empathetic are prime victims of narcissists because they can feed off these people's nurturing and loving energies. There is nothing that you did to attract this person. This person sought you out and deliberately hid their true colors from you. Narcissists are like chameleons. They change their colors to suit the environment so that they can gain as much benefit from the people and situations they encounter. This person knows that they cannot reveal their true colors upfront and needs to plot and scheme to get into relationships that gain them the highest values.

Women get into relationships with narcissistic men because these men strive to make a great first impression and hold this façade until they have thoroughly hooked these women. They study these women to learn their needs and wants out of a partner then adjust their behavior to fit those criteria. They typically come off as warm, generous, and attentive at the beginning of a relationship. They fool women into believing that they are the whole package. These people are master manipulators that have developed an art out of getting under the skin of women and inducing feelings that get women attached to them.

Even the most assured of women can fall for such a person because even though their intuition might blare warning sounds, this person figures out the things that make a woman feel most wanted, needed, and loved. Those are addictive feelings because at our core, everyone wants to find that person that feels like their other half.

Slowly but surely the narcissist reveals their true nature though because no one can hold onto a façade forever even if they wanted to. However, by the time that the red flags are apparent, the narcissist has sunk his claws so deep into the woman that she cannot get free easily. Her emotions are entangled and the future that the narcissist has made her believe is possible is in danger of ruination. This is why many women stay in such relationships even after the narcissist reveals his true nature.

Human beings are deeply social creatures and once we have formed an emotional attachment to another person, it is not easily dissolved and left in the past. We either become blind to this person's undesirable traits or excuse their behaviors. While logic may tell us to run in the other direction, our hearts can supersede these thoughts in an effort to maintain that connection. This makes moving on difficult, hence why the narcissist is able to reel us back in even when we try to dissolve the relationship.

Prolonged exposure to a narcissist also diminishes mental and emotional health and tarnishes self-image. This person belittles other people. This can be a full-frontal attack or so covert that it is only realized after the damage is done. The victim's self-esteem and self-confidence suffer while the narcissist has their ego stroked because the victim is likely seeking out their attention even after the maltreatment. The woman may feel that she is unworthy of true love and learns to accept this abuse.

Another reason it is so hard to let go of a narcissist relationship is because it is hard to accept that we have been fooled so completely by another person. We yearn to believe that at least some of the things we based that relationship on is true, so we stay to search it out.

Also, many women harbor the false belief that they can change or help a narcissist. No one but the narcissist can take the steps necessary to change themselves. Getting the help, they need means seeking the counsel of a mental health provider or a trusted doctor so that they can gain the tools to build their self-esteem and self-confidence. This means that the narcissist has to confront his or her faults and inner demons, and work from the inside out to balance their emotions and solve their mental anguish.

This is a difficult task to do and is not an overnight process by any means. But only after this is done can a narcissist be able to have healthy interactions with other people. I say all of this to stress that women the world over need to recognize that they need to work on themselves so that they can be happy and leave these narcissistic men to deal with their own inner demons because there is no fixing someone who does not realize that they are flawed in such a fundamental way.

The reasons for entering such a relationship are irrelevant at the end of the day. What truly matters is moving on. To do that, you need to stop blaming yourself. Accept that you were deceived by a master manipulator and pathological liar. You are not the first and you will not be the last.

The true blame falls on the narcissist but do not wait for this person to realize their faults and come to you with the closure you need. You need to claim that for yourself. You can start the process without an acknowledgement or apology from this person because that is part of your power as a strong woman. Now that you see past the lies and deceit, and understand the psychology of how this person hooked you, you can leave them in the past and move into the future where you are better able to spot similar people so that you defend your honor and worth.

Chapter 10 - Things a Narcissist Will Always Do In a Relationship

You can be able to tell if the person you are in a relationship with is a narcissist based on the kind of behavior, he/she exhibits throughout the duration of your relationship. Ideally, you want to be able to figure out if your boyfriend, girlfriend, or even an acquaintance has narcissistic tendencies as soon as possible so that you can sever ties with him/her before you are too invested in that relationship. Here are ten things that a narcissist will always do in a relationship.

He Will Try to Charm You

Narcissists can be quite charismatic and charming when they want something from you. If you are in a relationship with one, he will go out of his way to make you feel special in the beginning so that you trust him enough to let your guard down. As long as you are serving the purpose, he wants you to serve; the narcissist will give you a lot of attention and make you feel like you are the center of his world. If someone puts you on a pedestal during the early stages of your relationship, you should pay more attention to the way they act, just to see if they are faking it.

He Will Make You Feel Worthless

After you have been hanging out with a narcissist for a while, you will notice that when you have any sort of disagreement or argument, his first instinct is to dismiss you in a way that makes you feel worthless. He will criticize you in the sort of contemptuous tone that will make you feel dehumanized. When you disagree with ordinary people, you always get the feeling that your opinion matters to them, but with a narcissist, that is not the case. All the things about you that the narcissist claimed to like when he was charming you will somehow turn into negative attributes, and the narcissist will portray himself as a "saint" for putting up with those attributes.

He Will Hog Your Conversations

Narcissists are in love with the way people perceive them, so they will take every chance to talk about themselves. Whenever you try to have a conversation, the topic is always going to change, and it will suddenly be about them. It's never a 2-way conversation with a narcissist unless he is trying to manipulate you into thinking he cares about you. You will get to a point where you really struggle to get him to hear your views or to get him to acknowledge your feelings. When you start telling a story about something that happened to you at work, you will never get to the end of it because he is going to start his own story before you are done with yours. If you make comments on certain topics of conversation, your comments will be ignored, dismissed, or even corrected unnecessarily.

He Will Violate Your Boundaries

From very early in the relationship, the narcissist will start showing disregard for your personal boundaries. You will notice that he violates your personal space, and he has no qualms about asking you to do him favors that he has by no means earned. He will borrow your personal items or even money and fail to return it, and when you ask, he is going to say that he didn't know it was such a big deal to you — the point is to make you seem petty for insisting on boundaries that most decent people would consider reasonable.

He Will Break the Rules

The narcissist will break the rules that you set for your relationship, and other social rules, without any compunction. The problem is that sometimes, we are initially attracted to rule breakers because they seem to be "bad boys" or "rebels," but those traits are in fact tale-tell signs of narcissism. A person who breaks social norms is definitely going to break relationship rules because relationships are essentially social contracts. If someone is trying to charm you, but in your first few interactions, you observe that he cuts lines, tips poorly, disregards traffic rules, etc., you can be certain that you are dealing with a narcissist.

He Will Try to Change You

When you are in a relationship with someone, they are definitely going to change you in a few minor ways (often unintentionally). However, when you are dealing with a narcissist, he is going to make a deliberate and perceptible effort to change you, and more often than not, it won't be for the better. He will try to break you, and he will try to make you more subservient to him.

You will find yourself making concession after concession, until, in the end; any objective observer can tell you that you are under his thumb. He will cause you to lose your sense of identity so that you end up being a mere extension of him. When you get out of that relationship, you will find it difficult to figure out who you are as an individual because he would have spent the entire duration of the relationship defining and redefining you.

He Will Exhibit a Sense of Entitlement

The narcissist will demonstrate a sense of entitlement for the most part of your relationship. At first, he may seem generous and considerate just to draw you in, but after that, you will see his entitlement rear its ugly head. He will be expecting preferential treatment all the time, and he will expect you to make him a priority in your life (even ahead of your own career or your family). There will be a clear disconnect between what he offers and what he expects, and he is going to want to be the center of your universe.

He Will Try to Isolate You

Any narcissist who wants to control you and make you subservient to him understands that you have a support system of friends and family who won't stand by and let him harm you. So, one of the things he will do once he has faked affection and earned some of your trust is he is going to try and isolate you. He will insist that every time you hang out, you shouldn't bring anyone along. He will make up lies to drive a wedge between you and your friends. He will play into the conflicts that exist between you and your family members to make you lean on them a lot less. If you let him get rid of your support system, he will have free reign, and you won't stand a chance against his manipulation.

He Will Express a Lot of Negative Emotions

Narcissists trade on negative emotions because they want to be the center of attention. When you are in a relationship with one, he is going to be upset when you don't do what he wants, when you are slightly critical of him, or when you don't give him the attention he is looking for. He is going to use anger, insincere sadness, and other negative emotions to make you insecure, to get your attention, or to gain a sense of control over you. If someone you are dating throws a tantrum over minor disagreements or when you aren't able to give him attention, it means that he has a fragile ego, which is a clear sign that he could be a narcissist.

He Will Play the Blame Game

This is perhaps the most common indicator that you are in a relationship with a narcissist. He will never admit to any wrongdoing, and he will always find a way of turning everything into your fault. When anything doesn't go according to plan, he will always point out your part in it, even if he too could have done something to change the outcome of the event. He will never take responsibility for anything, and when he takes action to solve a mutual problem that you have, he will always make it clear that you owe him.

Chapter 11 - The Effects of Narcissism and Other Anti-Social Personality Disorders in Childhood

From a young age, we are shaped by the actions and behaviors of our families, neighborhood and community. Parents often have the greatest impact on children and how they are raised. Other family members can have a strong effect as well, especially if they take on a parenting role or become involved regularly in your life during childhood.

If you've been raised by one or two narcissistic parents, chances are you are more susceptible to dating someone who may exhibit these signs as well. Narcissism, as well as BPD, histrionics and anti-social personality disorders in a parent or parental figure shape a significant amount of our childhood development. These effects remain with us for years, including adulthood, where they have a major impact on how we interact with other people and form relationships. While we may be aware of the detrimental effects of narcissism and other anti-social disorder traits from our parent(s), we may not understand the reasons why or the presence of a personality disorder until much later in life.

How do know if your parent is a narcissist? Chances are, you may already have a suspicion. Before considering the likelihood that at least one or both of your parents or a family member is a narcissist or psychopath, it's important to evaluate their complete personality history and how they handled major events and relationships in life, including their interactions with you. Often, people draw conclusions based on a few traits they don't like. This is common with spouses, especially exes, when people refer to them as "my psycho ex-boyfriend/ex-girlfriend", which is an over-dramatization of the undesirable experiences they had prior to a breakup. It's easy to dismiss unpleasant behavior or an emotional outburst as "psycho" without any context because it places a convenient label on a person based on a specific incident or event. Making the determination of narcissism and similar disorders in a parent can be a difficult process, because they can be subtle or extreme, depending on the individual. The following traits are the most common you may notice in a parent from your childhood and/or currently:

• Did your parents have high expectations without any room for error? Did they pressure you to get an A+ after you scored an A, or pick on your flaws or perceived weaknesses? This is a common trait of a narcissist parent because they will project their insecurities onto their children, much like they do with their partners. They also try to "shine" through their kids. If their child wins the first place in a pageant or competition, they see the win as an extension of themselves, and will continuously expect their child to achieve this unattainable level of perfect constantly, without exception.

•   Did your parents compare you to other children? Were you simply not good enough? "You should be more like your sister" or "why don't you act more intelligent like your cousin" are examples of what you might hear from a narcissistic parent. If you experienced this, you're likely familiar with how stressful and difficult to experience this was during childhood, especially when your own siblings, cousins or the neighbor's kids are smarter, better looking or more skilled than you, according to your parents. This is how a narcissistic parent will devalue their child to coerce them into doing "better", so they can brag about them to their friends, family and look good. You are their source of pride and joy to others and the target of their harshest criticisms and anger behind the closed door. Any slight variation from what they want or expect can become a source of extreme stress, and eventually develop into anxiety and contribute to depression later in life, starting in the teens.

•   Regardless of how well you perform and far you go in life, achieving success, even beyond your own expectations, it will never be enough to a narcissistic parent. This can plague a child from a young age to adulthood and beyond, even where the toxic parent may not occupy an active part in your life. Adult children may still look for the approval of a narcissist parent, even if they fail to gain this acceptance over and again. It's a tragic cycle that only ends once you make peace with the fact that your parents will never truly accept you as you are, and always compare you to someone better. Why do they do this? They are insecure and lack self-esteem in themselves; any measure of success you achieve reminds them of their insecurities, which they exaggerate in their minds. While they stew in self-loathing, they target your success and achievements to make themselves feel better, which is akin to bullying.

• A narcissistic parent will want to shine, whether it's through their kids or on their own. They want center stage always, even stealing the attention from their own children, without regard for their needs. This often leads to different forms of neglect, where the child learns that they are not as important as their parents. This may prompt them to seek approval by making their parents feel proud of them, or accomplishing more, just for a small amount of affection.

• They will use guilt and remind you of everything they've done to help you, whether they contributed generously to your education or provided token favors and gifts. "You should be grateful for what I give you" or "without me, you would be nothing at all" are typical examples of how they will make you feel guilty for not doing or accomplishing exactly what they want. A narcissist can appear kind or generous at times if they feel that their "investments" will somehow pay off and make them look good or boost their status and appearance with others. "My son/daughter graduated just completed their doctorate" is something they want to share and boast about, not because they are proud of you, but because it boosts their image. They can have no involvement or contact with you for years, and upon learning of your success, they will use it to gain favor among their peers and social circle, saying things like "they get their looks/brains from me" or "they are just like me".

• Becoming sensitive and easily agitated is another example of how narcissists act around their children. They may be intolerant of specific practices or habits that are unimportant, to the point where they are suddenly angry or frustrated without good reason. You may feel as though you're walking on eggshells to avoid conflict, or become compulsive about checking your habits or tasks, to make sure you haven't left anything on the kitchen counter or returned the television remote control in the same exact position it's expected to be. Any deviation from their preference, as insignificant as it is, can be an unexpected source of tension that creates a constant state of anxiety and stress and making every effort to comply with their demands to avoid their tantrums and outbursts.

• Narcissistic parents lack empathy towards their children, and when they show any sign of care, it's often shallow and short-lived. They can hurl an insult or make an insensitive comment without any understanding of its impact on their child. If they are confronted with their behavior, they may respond with "I didn't mean that", "you're too sensitive," or "just get over it." This is hard to cope with at a young age when a child leans on their parent to acknowledge and understand their feelings. Most parents are aware of how certain actions or words can hurt and cause emotional pain in their kids, even to the point where they may become overprotective and careful. A narcissist mother or father isn't mindful of their actions and the impact they have on their children. Without any regard for their kids' emotions or feelings, they may cause their children to distance from them over time because the experience is too hurtful to deal with.

• Some narcissistic parents can become codependent on their children, expecting them to always be there, even to the point of being unreasonable. This can be difficult when their adult children have families of their own and have to divide their time between their parents and children. The expectations may exceed what is normally expected, and the parent may become angry and manipulative, using guilt to make them feel inadequate or as though they are never doing enough. Taking care of elderly parents is a kind and admirable sign of unconditional love, though when one or both parents are narcissistic, the appreciation is never shown, and unconditional love is never reciprocated.

• Narcissistic parents are neglectful of their children, especially when it comes to their emotional needs. They may provide for them materially and appear to have the perfect home and family when there is an emptiness inside. The children of narcissistic parents will always feel unwanted or as though they are an obstacle to what their parent wants. Instead of focusing on their child's wants and needs, the narcissistic parent will fixate their attention on success, advancing their career and their status in the community, only showing interest in their children when it makes them look good for a promotion or being complimented on having well-behaved kids.

• Children should always have the support and admiration of their parents, especially when they accomplish a goal or an achievement that they are proud of. When a narcissistic parent is jealous, they may instead degrade or insult their child's progress. This is a difficult experience for kids, who are not looking to compete with their parents, but rather, they are looking for approval and validation.

One of the most difficult and hurtful traits of a narcissistic parent is conditional love. They can appear to love their child or show a genuine interest, only to withdraw this affection, and in effect, place conditions on when they will love their child. This is one of the most challenging aspects of growing up with a narcissistic parent because it implies that we can be simply discarded and unworthy of love based on someone's superficial ideas and selfishness.

Chapter 12 - Techniques to Handle Narcissists

Now comes the difficult part! Deciding what to do with the narcissistic person in your life, and what the best outcome is. This can depend greatly on your individual circumstances as well as the person at hand.

Get Away

The most obvious, but by far the best piece of advice for dealing with narcissists that are not central to your life and are of no emotional significance to you is to not interact or deal with them at all.

Typically, extreme narcissists lack normal levels of empathy, don't pull their own weight, and tend to make the people close to them miserable within the space of a few weeks or months. They are unlikely to have a great deal of insight into their damaging behaviors and are unlikely to have an epiphany compelling them to change.

Relationships you could potentially cut off include not only romantic partners, friends and ex-colleagues, but also family. If you are not legally bound to remain in contact with someone – such as engaged in a business, joint ownership of property, administration of a will, or where a dependent is involved, then you have the potential to cut away if you need to.

Less drastic steps include taking a break or managing the situation. Breaks can help to gain clarity, but it depends upon the relationship at hand, and whether you deem it to be worth saving. If abuse is currently involved in the relationship, an immediate cut-off should be instigated, rather than attempting to make the best of it.

It's important to choose the people you spend time with wisely, because humans tend to adopt the characteristics of those around them. Professor Nicholas Christakis of Yale University explains this in terms of the ripple effect, whereby altruism and meanness ripple through networks of people, and be magnified. Whatever enters your system- including the actions of your peers, colleagues and family- will affect your personality development and outlook. Surrounding yourself with good people will make you behave in more kind and empathic ways.

Avoid the Inner Circle

If you need or want to keep a narcissist in your life, it is much safer to do so at a distance, rather than as part of their inner circle- who become privy to their chaotic changes in temperament. Creating justifiable distance (but remaining warm) allows you to be a welcome part of their life without suffering so many falls from grace. They may well start to think of you quite fondly. Get too close, however, and you may become an undervalued part of the furniture, without your own identity or boundaries to respect. In addition, you are giving more opportunities for your words and actions to be misinterpreted as threats or competition, and you are far more likely to have your fingers burned.

Whilst you may have identified the narcissist as a damaging individual, many people (particularly those under their control) will never be able to see the situation clearly. This can feel extremely unfair and unjust to those who can, particularly in family or romantic situations, if they are directly affected by narcissistic control, abuse or manipulation. The narcissist may be a master at making others look like "the bad guy," and may even have laid the groundwork for this future eventuality to further their control.

It is usually those people who "question" the status quo that the harmful narcissist finds most threatening, and subsequently suffer most acutely at their hands; as the narcissist feels compelled to bring them down to maintain their position. If the narcissist is a family member, particularly a parent, or a partner, this can be particularly damaging, with the victim often trained to unquestioningly agree or go along with the narcissist's opinions, to maintain their love and their favor. Those that follow receive their rewards, whilst those that question, are isolated, ridiculed and ousted, often labelled as a "black sheep," "troublesome" or "combative."

Avoid Narcissistic Injury

Sometimes, cutting the chord on a narcissistic relationship is not an option. You may feel you should at least try and continue a non-abusive relationship, in which case avoiding "narcissistic injury" is key to avoiding conflict.

In the minds of narcissistic people- both healthy and extreme- they are competent, have unique and special talents, and accomplished. In the case of healthy narcissists, any reasonable threat or challenge to these self-beliefs can be handled carefully, objectively, and in a proportionate way by the individual.

Threats to healthy narcissists don't include other successful or accomplished people- they may be positively competitive, but not derogatory. If a healthy narcissist takes a blow to their self-esteem, negative feelings may be processed without a melt-down or flying into a rage. Extreme narcissists, on the other hand, tend to exist in a world of hypervigilance. Any perceived threat or challenge is likely to be aggressively countered. Failing to do so could result in painful crashes to their self-esteem (narcissistic injury), as their opinion of themselves are overinflated, delicate and variable. This hypervigilance includes people they see as threatening, so it may be beneficial for you to lie low and purposely reduce the traits of your own that may make them feel competitive or badly about themselves.

Avoid Exposing Them

Exposing the narcissist and getting the "truth" out for all to see can be appealing and feel like the right thing to do. You may think this is the best solution for them, you and anyone else involved- that they will suddenly see clearly and take responsibility for changing their behavior. Forget about being right for a moment and bringing the truth to light.

Pointing out that the narcissist is not as wonderful as they think can result in a huge backlash that you then must be around and may not be able to escape. They are not ever going to agree with you, as they are tied to their elevated identity. Rather than changing their minds, they will be more likely to simply despise you for your opinions.

Avoid Showing Weaknesses

If you show a narcissist what it is that makes you vulnerable, or what it is that you really want, they may at some point use it against you when they want to manipulate you. Narcissists will frequently learn what it is that you want most from them and set about denying it so that you are in a constant state of "need." If a narcissistic mother does this, she may control her children through their neediness for her love. The same goes for a romantic partner. They'll ration your supply of what you enjoy most from them to keep you controllable and pliable.

If they know your greatest concerns or fears they may leverage these to manipulate you. They may even use you as a distraction from their own inner turmoil when they are experiencing crashing self-esteem, by needling you on your points of weakness, to make they feel strong again.

For example, an NPD manager suffering a meltdown of anxiety after a disastrous sales pitch may proceed to milk his staff for reassurance on his performance, whilst then moving the conversation on to subjects that he knows are extremely personal and emotional for them-transferring his fears to them and feeling better himself.

By not conceding any weaknesses to a narcissist and always taking a diplomatic "I know I'll be happy either way" approach, their power to bring you down whilst raising themselves higher is lost. This may take on the appearance of a game of cat and mouse, until eventually the narcissist must concede that you are not "easily pinned" or risk exposing themselves and being seen as a pessimistic and negative person.

Give Them an "Out"

You can give them the opportunity to stop playing manipulative games by offering them an "out" such as: "You're being uncharacteristically pessimistic today- you're usually such an optimist- is there anything wrong?" and in doing so call them to return to their "higher state of glory" without continuing their attack. Subconsciously, they may even be aware that you successfully navigated their manipulation and decide to give you a wider berth in future, or that they need to keep you on side.

If the attack is particularly vicious or nasty, avoiding emotions but maintaining a cool, calm and empathic approach can work well to bring them back around. Whether you believe it or not, providing those with a defense that effectively excuses their behavior will be much appreciated - as it helps them to avoid a crushing sense of shame and subsequent denial loops, and simply feel that they are understood and forgiven. You may even be surprised to find that this approach results in a voluntary concession and what may seem like the beginnings or a more responsible approach, but this is not something that should be anticipated or expected.

Don't Expect Fairness

Extreme narcissists are likely to be far more concerned with getting what they want, than ensuring that everyone is treated fairly. Reward their behavior rather than their words so that they only get what they want, when you get what you want too.

Extending credit or accepting promises from an extreme narcissist is a dangerous leap of faith that may not be rewarded. Lack of follow through is just as likely to occur because the narcissist forgets their agreements- their attention being consumed with themselves and their own concerns rather than remembering their obligations. Make sure that you get what they promise before you give them what they want. A quid pro quo approach may be insulting to some people, but to a narcissist they are likely to respect you for looking out for yourself.

They Want to Look Good

Understanding what a narcissist wants means that so long as you avoid triggering narcissistic injury, they may be able to be worked with. You may even be able to maneuver them, if you start to think like them.

Extreme narcissists really want to look good. If you can align what they want with what you want, you may be able to achieve great successes together. Alternatively, you may simply be able to manage and placate them to make your life easier or until you are able to leave the relationship.

Giving an extreme narcissist a way to be impressive if they do as they are told makes them easier to deal with, so long as you ensure you get what you want up front.

Chapter 13 - What is Codependency?

A healthy relationship is one where the partners have mutual respect. Although the individuals in a healthy relationship can function independently, they understand the need for interdependence, and they give each other the support they need to pursue personal as well as their collective goals. They treat the relationship like a partnership and indeed, that is what a healthy relationship is whether it is between lovers, family members, coworkers, or friends. There is a sense of shared and balanced responsibility emotionally, financially, and otherwise. And in the case of romantic relationships, emotional and physical intimacy is nurtured and grows because there is a healthy atmosphere of interdependency.

But when one partner in a relationship starts doing all the emotional heavy lifting, the relationship is lopsided and may likely end prematurely or continue to exist as an unhealthy one. This type of relationship has one person being dependent on the other while the other partner being codependent on the first.

There is no doubt that we all need each other to live truly and fully. However, when a person's sense of self tends to depend heavily on what other people think and feel, it has overstepped the boundaries of healthy human relations. People who live this way are known as codependents. They have surrendered their power to other people and live their lives following the whims and unpredictability of others. No matter how highly we regard the people in our lives, to give them control over us is unhealthy for our sanity and normal function. However, many people who give up their power do it unconsciously and find themselves trapped in relationships that seem impossible to wriggle out of.

What is Codependency?

Codependency simply means too much psychological or emotional reliance and attachment to someone who requires care and support as a result of ill health or addiction. A person who lets the behavior of someone they care for to influence them significantly to the extent of feeling responsible for controlling the other person is codependent. The codependent may have good intentions (to care and show compassion), but because of certain flaws in their thinking, they assume too much responsibility and do more harm than good in the process.

The actions and inactions of a codependent enables (or encourages) the behavior of the dependent. Instead of controlling the dependent, they end up encouraging their indolence, addiction, irresponsibility, and immaturity. For example, a mother who is "always there" for her delinquent son, may assume that she is protecting the son from harm. Unfortunately, her actions are only enabling her son to be more criminal-minded. But the damage is not just limited to the dependent. The codependent is usually left feeling frustrated and resentful because their "good deeds" are either not reciprocated or completely taken for granted.

Codependency is a behavioral disease that is learned over time. When it becomes ingrained, it can lead to self-destructive tendencies. A person who doesn't know when to stop making personal sacrifices can be misguided into willingly suffering for a lost cause. The intention may be noble, but the process is flawed. People can only change when they choose to and on their terms. But codependents can't seem to regulate their urge to give care because caring or helping others is their way of controlling other people. Unfortunately, this form of control can hurt them by making them lose themselves in the process of controlling others.

Codependents don't behave as normal clingy people do. They are not merely interested in making others love or need them. Instead, they tend to believe that their sense of self comes from how well others accept them. Typically, codependents plan their lives around their partner or the dependent. Their self-esteem and self-worth are tied to feedback from external sources, which is why they are preoccupied with approval-seeking behaviors.

The other person may be faced with issues of addiction, but the codependent is equally addicted to giving help even when it is uncalled-for. A codependent relationship usually has one partner (the codependent) making great personal sacrifices to please or keep the other partner satisfied. As a result, the codependent partner may endure an abusive relationship especially if the other partner is a narcissist.

Of course, not all dependents are narcissists. However, since narcissists are usually on the lookout for partners who tend to be excessively compassionate, many codependent relationships have the narcissist as the dependent. Although the word "dependent" may sound like a description for a timid person, it doesn't necessarily mean so. Narcissists are not timid, neither do they depend on their partners because they are weak. On the contrary, they are brave and bold (or appear to be so outwardly) and use that to lord over the codependent.

Since codependents can only have fulfillment (temporarily) from making others happy, it is not surprising to find them giving narcissists the attention they seek (even though they do so grudgingly most times). The codependent seeks approval from the narcissist, which they never get and continue to try harder in the vain hope that they can change the narcissist. On the other hand, the narcissist seeks admiration from the codependent, which they happily get, but feel unsatisfied with the inferiority or low self-esteem of the codependent. A narcissist will prefer to be in a relationship with a person they think of as equally superior to them. But because people with a great sense of self-esteem won't succumb to narcissists, narcissists grudgingly settle for codependents. In many cases, the unsatisfied feelings of a codependent can lead to frustration and resentment. But the unsatisfied feelings of a narcissist can result in verbal, physical, and emotional abuse.

Codependency can be relatively easier to treat compared to narcissism, which may be difficult to treat because it is caused by a complex mixture of known and unknown factors. However, it takes time, commitment, and patience on the part of the codependent for a sustainable recovery. Since codependency is a learned habit, treatment is usually in the form of psychotherapy, counseling, and other self-help methods not involving medications (unless the individual suffers from depression or other mental health conditions). It may be desirable for both partners (dependent and codependent) to get help at the same time. But this is not always the case. Codependents are usually hung up on the idea of getting help for others, so it is not surprising to find them wanting to make their partners change or get treatment. It is often not feasible to get someone to change, especially when they are not willing to do so. It even makes it nearly impossible if the dependent is a narcissist.

If you are codependent in your relationship, seek help with or without your partner. Your recovery does not depend on anyone else changing but you.

Causes of Codependency

Codependency is not a character or personality flaw; it is not a genetic trait either. It is a learned habit that usually starts early in an individual's life. The following factors are associated with the development of codependent behaviors.

- Living with a Mentally or Physically Ill Family Member

People who lived a significant part of their lives with and giving care to a constantly ill family member are prone to becoming codependent. They learn to put the sick person's needs ahead of their own and make huge personal sacrifices for them. Over time, such caregivers may begin to disregard their personal needs to fulfill the needs of their ill family member. Eventually, they can unconsciously reprogram their minds to hinge their sense of self-worth on the care they can give. Taking full responsibility for the sick person's wellbeing becomes an obsession – a form of control.

- Growing up with Dysfunctional Parents

Children who were raised in families where one or both parents abused drugs or misused some other substances are likely to develop codependent traits as adults. Growing up in such families and experiencing how their parent's irresponsible and behavior put the children in a position to take on caregiving responsibilities early on in life. Also, through constant harsh criticisms, harassments, mistreatments, and neglect, the children learn to put their parents' needs ahead of theirs. They grow up to believe that it is more important to give care to others than to oneself. These types of influences shape the child's psychological development and can lead to seeking codependent and dysfunctional relationships as adults.

- Growing up in an Abusive Family

Exposure to physical, emotional, and sexual abuse can cause severe traumatic experiences for young children. Children who grow in such abusive families where these experiences are a frequent occurrence are likely to live with these traumas throughout their lifetime. It is not uncommon for such children to enter into lopsided and abusive relationships as adults because that is their subconscious idea of what a relationship looks like.

Children who grow up in abusive families are likely to learn how to disregard or mute their feelings of anger and frustration to cope with the pain of abusive experiences. If carried into their adult years, they are likely to become codependents.

Chapter 14 - Powerful Self-Care Tips for Abuse and Trauma Survivors

Being a trauma survivor is an ambitious journey. Most of all, it provides us access to associate with other survivors who have already been where we are now. It's in those supporting communities where we come across the most recovery outside the treatment area. So as not to make the procedure overwhelming, I have chosen some significant self-care hints I feel most survivors of injury may gain from. Below are a few suggestions I've lived by; this may benefit the healing journey for those who have been through abuse and trauma. This article was featured The National Domestic Violence Hotline.

5 Powerful Self-Care Tips for Abuse and Trauma Survivors

As part of lifelong injury and abuse, I turned into a creative and energetic consumer of different procedures to cure myself. Additionally, I learned from a young age to talk to myself compassionately to offset the abuse I've experienced. I didn't understand it then, but I was staging what I afterward dubbed a "reverse discourse" contrary to my trauma - imitating the narratives of the numerous ways I was traumatized into powerful resources for transformation. Now, I assist survivors all around the world start the journey I started several decades back.

Positive affirmations. To purify our subconscious thoughts that have been influenced by the abusive phrases and activities we have experienced, we must purify our minds and decrease the negative, damaging automatic thoughts that might emerge within our daily life. These ideas stir self-sabotage and keep us from adopting all of the energy and service we must use to reconstruct our lives. A lot of these ideas aren't our own, but instead the voices of our insecurities and insecurities who still taunt us long after the abuse has stopped. As soon as we've been mistreated or bullied, we continue to abuse with what injury therapist Pete Walker calls the voice of the "inner critic." The most effective way I have reprogrammed my internal voice is by positive affirmations that I participate in daily. All these are positive affirmations tailored for specific insecurities and wounds. For example, if you've got any doubts about your appearance that your abuser has tried to instill in you, then a confident confirmation could softly interrupt the routine of ruminating within such unpleasant remarks by substituting the poisonous notion for an adoring one. A self-sabotaging idea about your appearance becomes "I'm beautiful, inside and outside," if the damaging emotion or thought surfaces. Among the very best methods for positive affirmations, apart from saying them, is "reverse discourse" that I talk about in my very first novel, The Smart Girl's Guide to Self-Care. Record your positive affirmations onto a voice recording program and then listen to them every day. Hearing your voice copying these affirmations every day -"I love myself," "I'm precious," "I'm worthy," "I'm beautiful" - is a compelling approach to emphasize that the story abusers have composed for you is wrong and exude that browbeating bully inside your head.

Heal the brain through your system. According to injury specialist Dr. Bessel van der Kolk, the author of The Body Keeps the Score, harm resides in our bodies in addition to our heads. Significantly, people find at least one kind of physical socket for the extreme emotions of despair, anger, and harm we are bound to sense in the wake of abuse and injury to fight the paralysis that accompanies harm, leaving us feeling stressed and frozen. I enjoy foreplay, yoga, dancing, cardiovascular activity, and jogging while listening to powerful songs or positive affirmations. Do something that you are passionate about and want to perform. Do not force your system to actions that you are uncomfortable with or that harm you. Employing physical exercise as a socket ought to be a procedure of self-care, not self-destruction.

Breathe. For abuse survivors who fight symptoms of PTSD or complex PTSD, careful breathing meditation and exercises are particularly beneficial in handling what Pete Walker requires for our "fight, flight, freeze, or fawn" answers to flashbacks and ruminating ideas. As an undergraduate freshman at school, I discovered how to meditate during my college's mindfulness applications. On my own, I researched hundreds of different kinds of meditations on the web and via podcasts - everything from self-compassion meditations to Chakra cleansing ones. I taught others to mediate for the very first time in a club meeting at college - and now, I do meditations for survivors of psychological abuse all around the world, to assist them in healing. Meditation is and has been among the most effective tools in my toolkit. Taking the time to watch our breath, whether for 5 minutes or an hour, can be hugely useful for handling our feelings and nonjudgmentally fixing our debilitating triggers. Additionally, meditation rewires our mind so we can mindfully strategize maladaptive reactions that keep us locked to the unfortunate occasion. If you've not meditated before and want to attempt it, I strongly suggest a program called Quit, Breathe and Believe, advocated for folks of all ages.

Channel your pain right into imagination. Art therapy is particularly valuable to individuals with PTSD since it allows survivors to seek out manners of expression, permitting them to make and integrate instead of self-destructing. According to van der Kolk, injury can influence the Broca's area of the mind that deals with speech. It may close down this region of the brain, disabling us from expressing what's happening. Allowing ourselves to say the injury in a somatic manner is vital because injury and the dissociation included with it might be tricky to express in words. After we are dissociated in the injury, our mind protects itself by providing us an outsider view into the injury, preventing us from our individuality, ideas, feelings, and memories linked to the injury. The mind will "divide" a traumatic occasion so it's easier to digest (Kalshed, 2013; Schuster, 2013). Since injury can detach us from our bodies and minds through procedures like depersonalization, derealization, and even dementia, the artwork will help us reintegrate the injury at which we were formerly disconnected in the encounter. As Andrea Schneider, LCSW, phrases it, expressive artwork could be a manner of "sparking the injury" that we have experienced. Whether it's painting, drawing, making music, performing crafts, and arts - it is crucial to publish the injury in different techniques

104

to engage both body and mind. I've used my different traumas to paint, draw, and write poetry, fiction, and articles regarding misuse to assist other victims. When we make something, we have the option of sharing our art with the world if it is a gorgeous painting or a publication. Exploiting our annoyance into imagination may be a life-changing encounter - both for ourselves and others.

Asking for assistance. In contrast to the popular view, asking for help doesn't make you helpless or powerless. It's a solid comprehension of your power to have the ability to seek out assistance and also be open to receiving it. Connecting using a bunch of aliens helped me tremendously to confirm and respect my adventures. It fueled my capacity to become self-compassionate and gave me a passion for assisting others in their healing journeys.

Sharing your story with other survivors can be extremely therapeutic and cathartic; however, if you're fighting with the consequences of injury, I highly suggest locating a validating psychological health practitioner who specializes in trauma and understands its symptoms as well as locating a support group of fellow survivors. Assistance from a mental health specialist during the procedure can ensure that you tackle your injury triggers at a secure area.

It's crucial to opt for a validating, trauma-informed adviser who will satisfy your wants and gently guide you with the proper treatment that covers the indicators and causes. You must be encouraged in a secure space using a trauma-informed adviser that will satisfy your wants and gently guide you with the right treatment for your situation. Some survivors gain from EMDR treatment, a treatment that lets them process their injury without being traumatized from the procedure. But a treatment that works for a single survivor might not operate the same for another depending on their particular symptoms, the seriousness of the injury, and the duration of time that an individual was traumatized. Make sure to go over your ideal treatment with your emotional health professional. As a nutritional supplement to treatment, you might want to also consult with low-cost or free mental health sources. During this journey of recovery from abuse and trauma, be confident you are self-compassionate on your own. A lot of harm survivors suffer from toxic shame and self-blame. Significantly, we must be gentle with ourselves throughout this journey, admit that we're doing our absolute best, and ask ourselves each day, "What is the most loving thing that I can do for myself right now?" There's no time limitation to healing and learning; there's merely the ability to change our hardship to success, one small step at a time.

Chapter 15 - How to Learn to Live and Love After Being with a Narcissist

Mistakes to Avoid

Don't Believe That Knowledge Alone Will Keep You Safe. That is only the first step, however. You had to implement new, unfamiliar, even unnatural behaviors just to regain some semblance of rationality so you could escape that narcissist, and therein lies the key to successful recovery.

Now one of the most important things you have to do is continue the momentum you started by leaving (or deciding to leave, if you have not yet left). Persistence in action is what will deliver you from the heart of darkness, now and in the future. You have to keep going, keep pushing, keep trying, and never let your guard down. This is a lot to take, and a lot to handle. But it beats remaining in an environment designed to eventually kill you. No one can survive in a toxic environment forever.

Now that you know you must keep being active in your recovery, one of the most important things you'll need to understand is that your conscious mind does not have the tools it requires to heal your emotional, psychological damage that was caused by the narcissist. As a survivor, you have inner trauma that's going to have to be dealt with. Knowledge about narcissism, and even acknowledging what has happened won't repair the wounds deep within your heart. You're going to have to seek help for this, such as seeing a therapist well-versed in recovery from narcissistic abuse or join a support group. Any place where you can gain the wisdom of others who have gone before you will help you on the road to healing.

It would be relatively easy to look at the narcissist and see only the sadist, the manipulator, the cruel person who hurts others for fun. This point of view is not entirely accurate. The narcissist's problems run much deeper, and she is not hurting for fun, she's hurting other people because compared to non-narcissists, her reactions, observations, and perceptions of other people and herself are woefully fractured.

Never Leaving Your Place of Shame. Many of us will struggle to get past this step, especially those of us who once prided ourselves on being strong, tough, and self-reliant. Many men struggle deeply with being victims of narcissism; this is not something that's supposed to happen to them, right? Wrong. Narcissists target anyone who peaks their interest, and they like to aim high. You were once capable of success, achievements, and love—and you will be, again, as soon as you get over blaming yourself for the abuse. You are not at fault—only the narcissist is.

Distraction, Instead of a Focal Shift. Further on we're going to talk about the need for a shift in focus while you recover. This is not the same as constant distraction. Keeping yourself from thinking about what happened is only prolonging both the pain as well as the healing.

You need to set aside some time on a regular basis to do some deep self-searching, and work on tackling recovery, one step at a time.

For however long we were in the relationship with our abuser, we did just this—distracted ourselves so we wouldn't have to deal with the terrible truth. Reworking your thinking patterns involves ditching this practice. While it was necessary at the time, it will work against us now that we are free of the narcissist.

Love on the Rebound. One of the most dangerous mistakes, replacing the missing "love", if it can be called that, with new love opens us to a particularly devious occurrence: meeting and becoming victim to yet another narcissist. At this stage in the game, you are not recovered, rebuilt, or reclaimed enough to be steady on your feet. You wouldn't be able to see the next abuser coming, even armed with the knowledge of what it takes to be a narcissist. You might accidentally (or on purpose) let slip about the abuse you suffered at the hands of your ex, and this could provide the new predator tons of ammunition in winning you over, sweeping you off your feet, then controlling your every move as both your savior and your new commander.

Additionally, you might have a lot of dark feelings after your traumatic experience—even if the new love is a genuine, well-meaning person, do you want to expose them to all the anger, resentment, and pain you've had to hide for so long? It's in there, even if you believe you've let it go. Only time and self-work can get it out, and so early on in your healing process is not the time to begin a new romance.

Don't Stalk the Narcissist. Of course, we don't do this because we want them back (usually), but because we're afraid. We want to keep up a perimeter of defenses and being pre-emptive and going on the offensive to see what the narcissist is up to seems perfectly natural, and it is. However, it also opens you up to contact. You must steadfastly adhere to the No Contact rule if you want to survive recovery and get your life back.

In addition, you might catch a glimpse of the person we call "The Replacement". The narcissist loathes being alone; she must have someone to feed her need for narcissistic supply or she will quickly self-destruct, so in your absence, she will find another victim. If you were to watch this play out on social media, you would be devastated and horrified to see that the exact process of "love-bombing", down to the places the narcissist goes with their new beau, to important proclamations of love and events they post about, almost exactly match yours when your relationship was in its inception. This can cause feelings of jealousy and hurt, even if we believe that we absolutely despise our former abuser. We might be tempted to reach out—perhaps tricking ourselves into believing that we are burying the hatchet. Even a simple message of "Congratulations, I'm so happy for you" can lead to terrible consequences. In two months', time, the narcissist might be back at your door, remembering that you still hold a place for them in your heart.

Rebuilding Your Self

This may seem like an impossible task, or at least, a daunting one. How does one go about the business of rebuilding self? To start, you need to quickly and firmly establish boundaries.

You are on your own, now, and that's a very good thing. There's only you to call the shots and make the rules. Start by listing what your boundaries must be:

• No one purposefully hurts you and gets to stick around.

• Your home is off-limits to violence and rage.

• Your body is your own; no one may violate it without dire consequences.

• You are prepared and willing to defend yourself and your loved ones.

• You know who you are—nobody gets to ridicule or question that.

• It is perfectly acceptable to say "no".

• You do not owe anyone your time, your attention, or your intimacy.

• You will adhere to the No Contact rule; no acceptations.

Because you are reacquainting yourself with what it means to have boundaries, it's important to take things slowly with new friendships, and leave dating until you've healed much more. Practice moments of boundary-enforcement during moments you're comfortable. If a social setting is too much for you right now, give yourself permission to opt out.

Reclaiming Your Reality

Forgive yourself and seek reminders of who you are. This is another time-consuming process and should never be rushed. Don't allow so-called friends and family members guilt you into "getting over it"; this is especially true for men recovering from abuse. Take as much time as you need and tell those who would push too hard to take a hike. This is an important first step in recovering yourself. You were a strong, capable person once, and you will be again. The first thing you need to do is treat yourself with respect, and demand that others in your close circles do, too.

Seek out friends and family who were close to you during the good times before you met the narcissist. Ask them to help you; perhaps plan a trip to a place you had some good times or re-read articles or stories you wrote that garnered praise. Pull out old sports trophies and look through yearbooks and albums. You are on a mission to find you. You're out there somewhere, waiting to once again live happily. The narcissist never new you—they never even saw you. Don't be afraid to like yourself again; it's necessary to achieve success and joy in life.

Redefining Your Belief System

Understand that a part of you knew that abuse was happening, and don't think less of yourself because of it. It's time to acknowledge the truth of what happened to you:

- You were tricked (because the other person is a narcissist).

- You were lied to (because the other person is a narcissist).

- You were manipulated (because the other person is a narcissist).

- You were hurt (because the other person is a narcissist).

- You were abused (because the other person is a narcissist).

The reason for the repetition is to help you get it into your head that there is only one reason these things happened, and that reason is listed above. You did not deserve to be hurt. You did nothing that warranted the abuse. You are simply not to blame.

Most people do not abuse others. There are so many people out there who would never dream of hurting you, who at the very least would show you a minimum of respect, and at the most would love you for the person you are, not the shadow they wish to torment. What you're doing now is strengthening yourself, so that you can once again believe that there's good in the world. Always remember, take this process one step at a time, and don't feel as if you're not making process fast enough.

Chapter 16 - What is Narcissistic Abuse Syndrome?

Narcissistic Abuse Syndrome is the deep array of psychological abuse one suffers from a narcissist. It is not as random or sporadic as narcissistic displays in passing or from a friend of a friend or acquaintance; but it is usually suffered when in a relationship with someone, or if you have formed a deep bond over a longer period of time. There is an element of karmic interplay involved in NAS, as the sufferer always unconsciously enters into some energetic and karmic entanglement.

If you are divorcing or taking the steps to divorce, then you most likely have NAS or suffer from some of its symptoms. The symptoms are many and there are many sociopathic and psychopathic tendencies displayed by the narcissist. NAS is arguably one of the most extreme forms of narcissistic abuse, or narcissism in its optimum. It is essentially a condition triggered by being in a "warzone" with a narcissist who continuously seeks to take control and command over you. Your thoughts, beliefs, emotions, will, mind and whole being are no longer your own. You are instead 'owned' by the narcissist and entrapped in their games.

It is an often-indescribable attack on the spirit, psyche, soul and personal identity. Being a sufferer of NAS can leave you feeling abused and with some form of PTSD. Your psyche is under constant assault and name calling, belittling, mind games and gaslighting are present and extreme.

Gaslighting

To start, if you suffer from Narcissistic Abuse Syndrome you will almost certainly be gaslighted. The narcissist will attempt to erase you from their existence in a way which makes you question your own sanity, intentions, abilities and self- worth. Your self- esteem will plummet, and you may suffer with severe depression or anxiety. Gaslighting is making you question your reality. You could be the most selfless, sincere, genuine, kind, giving, patient, compassionate and empathetic of beings, yet with NAS you will doubt all of these qualities.

There is also a question of being believed. It can be very hard to stand strong in your own truth and clarity as the narcissist will attempt to distort truths and "tell stories" to some of your closest friends and family.

Emotional Abuse

The emotional abuse suffered at the hands of a narcissist is on par with the psychological and mental abuse when dealing with a psychopath or sociopath. They use language in specific ways with intentions of capturing and imprisoning your mind and will. Emotional manipulation and all its connotations are most extreme in NAS. In fact, if someone was asked to picture the most severe forms of emotional manipulation, the characteristic of Narcissistic Abuse Syndrome would be the optimal.

Deep and Severe Manipulation

Connected to emotional abuse is the deep and severe levels of manipulation present. Referring back to the use of language; mental, emotional and psychological manipulation will be apparent, frequent and often. The victim and sufferer will not know where to turn or how to escape from such extreme exertions of manipulation. Friends, family and mutual acquaintances will even be turned and swayed. One key thing to know is that narcissists are incredible story- tellers. They will use your thoughts, desires, possessions, self- esteem, willpower and own strength reserves for their own gain.

Betrayal

Narcissists are experts at betrayal. There is no limit to the amount of pain, suffering and deception a narcissist can exhibit. Furthermore, they simply don't care. They lack empathy to the point of sadism and are happy to intentionally inflict deep trauma and betrayal on those who love and care for them. Linked to this is the aspect of bullying. You may not only be lied about and betrayed in this sense, but also bullied, threatened and made to feel severely weak or inferior through words and speech. This is a complete betrayal of your trust, of your heart and your sincerity, and can further leave you feeling completely isolated, victimized and traumatized.

Psychopathic and Sociopathic Behaviors

Extreme narcissists such as those who cause NAS often display sociopathic and psychopathic tendencies. A psychopath will do everything in their power to run you over, going out of their way intentionally to make sure that the utmost chao was caused. They will not only blame you for being in their way, but they would laugh; even backtracking to make sure they haven't missed a toe or fingertip.

This may seem like an extreme analogy, yet it portrays the type of energy and hidden motivations present in narcissists, sociopaths and psychopaths. Although narcissists may seem like the less extreme one out of the three, the main point is that they still show signs and actions-behaviors of socio- and psychopaths. Quite simply, Narcissistic Abuse Syndrome is as severe as they come.

Zero Empathy

It has already been mentioned but it still can't be stressed enough. Narcissists have zero empathy, meaning that they also feel no remorse for their evil deeds. They are egocentric, never apologize, don't know how to apologize; are expert story- tellers, present themselves as having high morals, are untruthful and manipulative, have superficial charm and an imposed sense of (false/ fake) social grace or philosophy, and feign like, love or care to get what they want. They can make themselves appear as the hero with superior morality when in reality they are evil, heartless and cold inside. An extreme narcissist truly has no shame or problem with ruining someone else's life.

Post- Traumatic Stress Disorder (PTSD)

Finally, one of the major results of being on the receiving end of Narcissistic Abuse Syndrome is the development of PTSD and related symptoms. It may be easy to want to shrug off the severity of NAS, see the victims or sufferers as dramatic or attention- seeking, or generally downplay the situation for what it is; however, those who suffer with real cases of Narcissistic Abuse Syndrome go through real psychological, mental and emotional abuse.

Some of the consequences of NAS in relation to PTSD can include: -

- Nightmares, flashbacks or recurring memories.

- Physical- emotional reactions and responses.

- Trauma, both on the surface and deeply buried.

- Avoidance of other people and a detrimental desire for excessive solitude.

- Intrusive thoughts, emotions, memories and manipulations.

- Negative and anxiety- ridden mindset.

- Negative and destructive/ harmful self- image and image about the world.

- Isolation and extreme detachment from friends, family and peers.

- Insomnia, anxiety and stress disorders.

- Fear to be oneself. Irrational and delusional fears.

- Extremely low self- worth, self- esteem and confidence.

Of course, these are some of the more extreme cases of being a sufferer of NAS, however they are still able to show up. Usually these symptoms and PTSD related tendencies present themselves over a longer period of time, once the chance to heal and begin a path to recovery has passed (or is in later stages).

Chapter 17 - Healing from a Narcissistic Abuse Syndrome

Healing requires the rebirth of ourselves. Some people think that they need to return to the person who they were prior to bonding with the narcissist. It is actually more important to become a different person than we once were. First, we can no longer be who we used to be. The narcissistic abuse has enabled us to grow and mature in many ways. We used to be mature about narcissistic abuse, and now, we are knowledgeable about its negative effects. Secondly, if we were to return to our former state, we would still be vulnerable to bonding with another narcissist. This is definitely not the goal of overcoming narcissistic abuse. We want to learn from our mistakes, and we want to make wiser choices going forward.

We must unsubscribe from the narcissist's theory that the world is a hostile place. This is the only way that we can open ourselves up to trusting others and realizing our own potential in the world. If we remain rooted in this theory, then we remain vulnerable to the narcissist's skewed reality instead of creating our own.

We must stop relying on other people to define us. It is a natural instinct to size other people up and to compare ourselves to others. This instinct was used in an age where we had to fight for food and for our own survival. Inner strength is actually more useful now, and thus we should look internally to define who we are. We can adjust how we behave and dress if we agree with others that we need to change something, but we should be comfortable with who we are in our own skin. We should not feel the need to change for others, and we should be comfortable withstanding up for ourselves when someone else is exerting an opinion on us that we do not agree with.

We must expose ourselves to new experiences in order to push out the negative past experiences. These new experiences will retrain our brains and improve our primitive internal mechanisms that help us to make unconscious split-second survival decisions. If we remain 'stuck' in the past, our responses to stressors fall back on those outdated ideas that we learned from childhood. The newer experiences you have, the better your odds are at erasing those old reactive mechanisms that were maladaptive.

We must ignore the negative and pessimistic inner critic inside ourselves. Our parents constantly told us what we can't and shouldn't do. This inner critic stops us from truly enjoying our lives. Stop listening to your critic. Become mindful of those in-the-moment decision-making process. Release the grip that the adults in your life had on you. Realize that they were imperfect and sometimes much too critical or judgmental of others.

Explore what your morals and values are, then examine each decision or option to ensure that you achieve personal growth while still adhering to your own set of standards for yourself. Don't blindly accept the morals and values of others. Make sure your morals and values still make sense to you, and the way you would like to live your life.

Explore your world to see what you like and don't like. Don't be afraid to make mistakes, to fail, or to get dirty. Look at each exploration exercise as a journey, not a destination. Even if you learn what not to do the next time around, you still learned something! You might simply realize that you don't like doing a certain hobby or activity. Each experience that you go through helps you to get that much closer to finding out who you truly are! When we fail, sometimes even a funny story can be shared later from our failures.

We must realize that we cannot control other people. We must learn to fully accept the fact that they are wholly imperfect human beings. They will make mistakes and let us down at times. We must learn that we can still get our needs met from others by enjoying the good parts of another person while allowing them to deal with their own negative traits. They are working on themselves and their personal growth on their own time, just like we are working on ourselves and our own personal growth. We should not even attempt to rush them on their journey and vice versa.

We must go no-contact or low-contact with negative persons in our lives who aren't able to look past their own pain and negative experiences in order to help us reach our goals. A person who cannot be supportive of another usually has a toxic inner voice and cannot force themselves toward their own personal growth. This is not our problem, and we should not take it personally when another person cannot support us toward our goals. We can choose to hang around people who are seeking growth, as well as those who seek to inspire us. Positive people can help us to improve our own personal growth by mentoring and encouraging us.

We must strive to be the best role model that we can be in order to help others to become their best. We must avoid stooping to another person's level when he or she isn't being mature and stable. If we stoop to another person's maturity level, it can either get us into legal trouble, drive us to traumatize or bully another individual or cause regret or resentment.

If we seek to be the mature one, other people might improve their own behavior unconsciously while they are around us, but they will do so only if they are able and ready to be mature. People with mental health problems or personality disorders may never act maturely, and we must accept that they cannot control some parts of their behavior that inflicts pain on others. We can, however, choose not to let their behavior affect us.

We must realize that other people with a critical opinion or a sharp tongue have a toxic inner voice that plagues them. We must accept that this is neither our fault nor our responsibility. If they indicate an opinion, we can compare it to our view of ourselves. We can still be okay with ourselves even when someone else is not okay with us.

We must realize that our anxiety can sometimes be a waste of our time. It is a primitive state of reactivity that is used to watch out for dinosaurs that are about to eat us. We must weigh the warning signs, and we must determine which ones we should truly consider against those which should be discarded. We must realize that if we are always feeling anxious, something in our life might need to change in order to become emotionally healthy again.

Don't ignore the signs of anxiety. Even when one's anxious reactions are over-sensitive and faulty; they sometimes warn us that a relationship isn't really healthy for us.

Test your anxiety. Find a place that calms you. Meditate there. Get in touch with your thoughts and feelings. Then, return to your friends and your family. Who causes your anxiety to return? Is this person critical, unsupportive or invalidating toward you? Do you feel better when you are not around that person? Then, why are you still sticking around? Would it truly hurt your life to choose not to be around them? Are you only around them due to a sense of obligation or a sense of guilt? Are you only around them to seek their approval?

If so, maybe the relationship is a negative one. Maybe you would be better off without this toxic relationship in your life. This test can be applied to parents, family members, significant others, bosses, coworkers, and friends. There are healthy people in the world. Surrounding yourself with healthy people will make you feel much better emotionally. It might also decrease your anxiety level significantly.

We must treat ourselves with love and kindness. We must re-parent ourselves in a new way. We must realize that our parents were not perfect, and we owe it to ourselves to pick up the slack where our personal growth is concerned. It is our own responsibility to fill in wherever they left off. We cannot keep going back to them continuously seeking validation and guidance. The purpose of parenting is to give a child enough tools to teach them how to fill in their own gaps in knowledge, life skills and education later in their life. The child must go out into the world and make something of his or her own life once he leaves the nest. This is the next part of our journey, and we must prove to ourselves that we can do this just as we were intended to.

We must realize that we only have one life to live. When we don't seek personal growth and learn from our mistakes, we may grow old, feeling regret and resentment. We must realize that life is messy, and that we must use the good and the bad parts to improve ourselves and to grow as strong and persistent human beings. We must learn how to roll with the punches in everything that we do so that we can become resilient.

To be resilient is to be powerful when others are not. The smallest and most primitive life forms continue to evolve and change over time in order to become resilient to their environment, and we should not allow other people to prevent us from becoming resilient. Once we are resilient, we are sheltered from some of the hurts and pain that others experience.

Consider your genetics and your diet. Some of us are prone to anxiety, depression, emotional lability, and other personality quirks that cause us distress. Still, others are sensitive to free glutamates (milk and soy) in their diet which drastically increase their anxiety level through something called excitotoxicity. Those who have Autism Spectrum Disorder, Asperger's Syndrome, Schizoid Personality Disorder, Social Anxiety, Anxiety, Depression and Schizophrenia traits running through their family lineage are especially prone to diet-induced anxiety, mood swings and learning deficits.

There are supplements that reverse the damage done by excitotoxicity and free glutamates in your diet. Some of them are glycine, l-theanine, and NAC. L-theanine is especially helpful in stopping anxiety, even in people with Complex PTSD who have had childhood trauma and relationship trauma. Check with your doctor before trying any new supplements.

Strive to work through the trauma in your life and to learn from your past mistakes. The brain needs a resolution to the trauma in order to learn how to make better decisions in the future. If you find yourself repeating bad patterns of the past, it is because your brain is either still trying to resolve the past trauma, or because your brain learned a maladaptive way to deal with the same set of circumstances. If something isn't working, try something new to break the cycle of old habits and maladaptive coping mechanisms. Try to consciously retrain your brain when it learns things the wrong way. Note carefully, this doesn't make you faulty, it only makes you human!

Chapter 18 - What is Gaslighting?

Gaslighting is a form of mental abuse, and it is commonly used by narcissists. The term itself was pegged in 1938 because of a play. The play portrays a man attempting to make his wife insane by messing with the lights inside of their home. The wife in this play tries to point it out to her husband, and he completely denies that the lighting within the household is changing at all. She starts to question herself, and he gains control. He is gaslighting her, and this is a brilliant example.

Many people deal with narcissists on a daily basis; however, it is surprising how many don't understand what gaslighting is. Gaslighting is one of the narcissist's favorite tactics to get complete control and power within their relationship. It abuses their partner and makes them second guess every thought and idea that crosses their minds.

Sometimes you are dealing with a narcissist, and you have no choice about it.

For instance, if they are a parent or family member, it is likely you can't rid yourself of the burden that is them. Narcissism can also be experienced in romantic relationships, as well as one's of a friendlier nature. Realistically, any relationship in your life could involve a narcissist, and each one is going to be a challenge to deal with. In fact, it is not only hard to deal with. It is oftentimes hard to recognize.

Narcissists have huge egos, and they only know how to love themselves. They will go to great lengths to have people perceive them in a certain way. They often tell stories of grandeur and think that there is no one better than them. Most narcissists are charismatic and can draw the attention of a crowd very easily. This can make it easy to fall for them and for them to gain control of you and your life. Recognizing a narcissist early on is the best defense against them.

If your partner ever repeatedly tells you that you are making things up or that you are remembering something incorrectly, it is likely that they are trying to gaslight you. This happens slowly over the relationship until the victim can't understand reality as it actually is. If you are being affected by gaslighting, it is common to find yourself questioning reality, your relationship, or possibly your own level of sanity. These are all signs of gaslighting.

This tactic is not only a form of mental abuse, but it is also a form of emotional abuse. When a person suffers from emotional abuse, it will take a toll on every aspect of their life. It is likely that they will have very low self-esteem. It is also common for those who suffer from emotional abuse to have problems with anxiety and depression. They often feel a sense of helplessness. In a gaslighting situation, they will become dependent on their narcissistic partner in every way. They start to accept the abuse as something that is normal and acceptable.

As noted, emotional abuse causes a lot of damage throughout their entire life. It is likely that they will question or not understand their own feelings. Additionally, it is likely that they will not trust their instincts, and they may even question their sanity. When these types of behaviors become an everyday occurrence, it puts all of the power and control into the hands of the narcissist. Once someone is no longer able to trust their own thoughts and ideas, it is much more likely that they will stay in an abusive relationship regardless of how terrible it is for them and their well-being.

The victim of gaslighting will, obviously, suffer, but so will the people that care about them.

Victims of this type of manipulation withdraw from the people they love, and that love them. They no longer trust what their most trusted assets have to say or what they think. Oftentimes, their relationships with anyone other than the narcissist will dissolve completely. This is painful and has a negative impact on everyone that cares about the victim. Trying to make the victim understand that what is happening is not right is almost impossible. This is especially true in terms of narcissistic relationships that have been going on for some time.

In addition, gaslighting is exceptionally effective in keeping a person under the narcissist's thumb. Mental and emotional abuse are ways for the narcissist to gain power within the relationship. They will gain control by any means necessary, even at the expense of their partner's happiness and well-being. Gaslighting is only one of the many forms of manipulation that the narcissist will use to maintain the life that they find suitable.

The effects of gaslighting do not happen overnight. It takes quite a bit of time and is typically quite gradual. In the beginning, their tactic may just look like simple misunderstandings. However, over the course of time, the abusive behavior will become continuous.

People on the outside of the relationship may be able to see the pattern of it, but it is unlikely that the partner being affected by it will be able to see this perception.

There are several reasons that the abused party will not be able to understand it when their friends, families, or loved ones try to tell them what is actually happening. Most narcissists will do their best to isolate their partner, which can lead to breakdowns of important relationships in the inability to hear what the people that truly care about them have to say. Victims of this type of use can also become extremely anxious or confused. This can make talking to them extremely difficult.

Depression is another element that comes along with gaslighting. People tend to disassociate with what is actually going on around them. Additionally, they may experience a lack of trust with people that care about them the most.

One of the saddest things about being in a relationship with a narcissist that uses gaslighting tactics is that eventually, the partner that is being abused will feel as if they absolutely need the narcissist to survive. Due to the fact that they cannot define true reality, they feel that they need their narcissistic partner to define it for them.

This makes the situation insanely difficult to get out of. It takes a lot of time and effort to help somebody open their eyes and realize that the person they love the most is actually abusing them and taking advantage of them.

Gaslighting not only manipulates people, it, realistically, is also a form of brainwashing. It lays seeds of doubt in the victim in every area. They won't be able to perceive the world as an individual, they may lose their identity completely, and it is likely that they feel very little self-worth. The thoughts, statements, and accusations of the gas lighter are consistently falsifications that are deliberate.

Their intention is thought out to make the person they are dealing with feel crazy, and thus, the narcissistic gas lighter holds all of the power and control within the confines of the relationship.

It does not matter how intelligent you are when it comes to gaslighting. If you do not see the signs and take action quickly, it is very likely that you will succumb to the wishes of the narcissist in your life. This is due to the fact that it can be hard to recognize. There are misunderstandings in every relationship due to poor communication or simple human errors of memory, so it can be easy to brush off the signs of gaslighting, especially in the beginning.

There are a variety of different signs that you are dealing with a narcissist that is using gaslighting tactics.

For now, simply know that if you notice constant miscommunications where you are the one in the wrong, it is possible that you are dealing with someone that actually means you mental and emotional harm. You must remember that this form of manipulation is a slow process. When you are aware of the experiences you face, by being present in the moment, it can offer you the protection you need to not proceed in a relationship with someone who utilizes gaslighting.

The narcissist loves the tactic of gaslighting because it is so hard to perceive. Tools like accusations, denial, lying, and misdirection are all used to throw the person they are focused on off the trail of truth. It often leaves them feeling as if the issues they bring forth are simply part of their imagination. Additionally, they end up feeling like everything is their fault because of the things that the narcissist says and does. Gaslighting truly can make a person feel insane.

Chapter 19 - Gaslighting – How to Avoid Gaslight Effect

Dealing with a narcissist is anything but easy. They are manipulators and tend to have their course of action already thought out. It is important that if you have to deal with a narcissist on a daily basis that you understand this as it can help you prepare yourself in how to deal with them and shut them down. Taking the time to step back and see what they are doing is key. When you understand the path that the narcissist is trying to get you to take, it can better prepare you to deal with it in a way that makes you feel comfortable and allows you to stick to your beliefs and morals.

Having a plan to deal with the narcissist in your life is excellent. This will allow you to be proactive in your approach with them instead of reactive.

Obviously, the narcissist is always looking for the reaction, and if you deny them that you are taking steps in the right direction toward shutting them down. Thinking ahead will allow you to keep up with the game that they are playing.

Stepping into an emotional engagement with a narcissist is never a good idea. You will always lose. They are excellent at sucking people into their chaos through emotions, and once you are there, it is very hard to get out. Through emotions, they will try to confuse you so they can have the upper hand. This is oftentimes done with gaslighting techniques. Instead of allowing a power struggle to occur between you and the narcissist in your life, you should remember to disengage. Don't allow them to get a rise out of you, which is exactly what their intention is so that they can take advantage of your heightened emotions.

Narcissists always want to be the center of attention. They want to be seen and heard. You can use this to your advantage. The behavior of a narcissist is oftentimes childlike. They may succumb to tantrums or outbursts so they can get their way. Instead of paying attention to the outburst, pay attention to what they are saying. Once you understand what the problem is that they are facing, you should simply let them know that you hear them.

You should also then reiterate back to them whatever it is that they just said. This gives them the fix they need to calm down and move on to the next thing and can save you a lot of trouble in the long run.

To be fair, everyone wants to be heard; however, with the narcissist, it is a thing that is extremely important. Their desire to be seen and heard is the same as a drug addict's desire to use drugs. So, by showing them that you are listening and that they are heard, you can quickly control some of their abhorrent behavior that, if handled differently, can become abusive to you.

Another great way to shut down the narcissist in your life is to say nothing at all. Narcissists tend to try and start altercations. They love them because arguments are opportunities to break you apart and gain more and more control. They will use insults, among other things, to ensure this happens. It can be hard to say nothing when they are saying things that are one hundred percent untrue, but you need to understand that you will never be able to change their mind, so responding or acting emotionally is going to have the opposite effect than the one that you desire.

If the narcissist is in a disagreement with you, and you have done your best to make your point, but no agreement can be reached, you simply need to stop talking or even walk away. Be aware this could make them lash out even more as they get a thrill out of the fight. Understand that there is no dealing with them at this point so simply stopping is the best way for you to shut them down.

The narcissist in your life is going to be one of the biggest liars, you know. The sad part about it is that the more they lie, the more they start to believe their lies to be the truth. They fool themselves just as much as they try and fool everyone around them. You may have tried to call your narcissist out on their lies before and likely it failed miserably. It frequently leads to anger or major insults. The narcissist has a false ego and that ego cannot be called out without repercussion. Instead of calling them out on their lies, it is better to play along all the while knowing the truth.

Using statements like "I believe you" and "I trust what you are saying," even if you don't, will allow you to find the end result that you are looking for. If the narcissist feels that you are falling for their lies, you will be able to traverse the choppy waters more easily. Stay calm and think before you speak. The outcome will be much better than if you try and point out the blatant lies that are flying out of the narcissist's mouth.

We all face difficult situations in life, and if you are facing one with a narcissist as your partner, it can be exceptionally daunting. When they feel that they are no longer in control, it can cause the narcissist to become anxious, aggressive, or panicky. This could lead to a blow-up that you obviously want to avoid. If you are facing a difficult situation with a narcissist, avoid telling them that you will handle it. This gives you the control and sends them over the edge. Instead, use reassuring phrases like, "Everything is going to be just fine." This will help you avoid negative outbursts.

Narcissists are very much like children in a lot of ways, and when you take that into consideration, it makes it easy to understand why the above phrase is going to be helpful. You can even take it a step further and tell your narcissist why and how everything will be ok. Reassuring the narcissist can help alleviate their insecurities and make them much easier to handle.

Avoiding an argument with a narcissist can be insanely difficult. Sometimes you simply need to validate the way they are feeling to truly avoid it. They may be going on and on about a small thing that has irritated them, and you are witnessing them start to lose control, which means it is about time for them to take it out on you.

Taking a moment to remind them that they are better than the situation and smart enough to handle it all can help calm the emotions down so you can move on to other things without ending up in a blowout argument.

Sure, this may seem a bit manipulative, but realistically to handle a narcissist, sometimes you need to play their game. Keeping the upper hand without them knowing is difficult but also advantageous. In normal day to day life, you don't just say things to get what you want, but sometimes, when handling a narcissist, it really will be your best course of action.

Anyone that has dealt with a narcissist knows that they do not like to be told what to do. In fact, if they are told what to do, especially by the person they are trying to control, it will almost always lead to a meltdown. So, another great strategy to shut the narcissist down is to make them think that your instruction is their idea. Ask them to do something and then back it up with examples of why they will like doing it.

Narcissists need to be the center of attention, so that means they also need everything to be their idea. They need the credit. By giving them a suggestion rather than flat out telling them what to do, you will likely find more success in them actually doing it and fewer outbursts.

It is understandable if you feel like these tactics are a bit manipulative and below how you would normally handle things. The thing you have to remember is that the narcissist does not believe that they have any flaws. You are not dealing with an average member of society, and this means sometimes you are going to have to play their game. Otherwise, you will likely end up consumed by their chaos and you will be giving them all the control, which is dangerous for your own personal well-being.

Another thing you can personally do to help you deal with a narcissist and shut down their cruel tactics is to look for a professional that understand Narcissistic Personality Disorder. When you are dealing with a narcissist, you need to have a good support system. A support system will help you deal with the toxicity of your situation, and it will also help you remember that you are not crazy.

If you have been in a relationship with a narcissist for a long period of time, you may not be in tune with your actual thoughts, emotions, feelings, desires, or even personal needs. Speaking to a professional about what is happening in your life with a narcissist can give you the tools you need to cope with the situation and find your way back to yourself.

Unfortunately, if you are still with the narcissist, you will likely need to keep this professional support a secret, or they will simply tear you apart over it.

Realistically, one of the very best ways to shut a narcissist and their gaslighting behaviors down is to refuse to argue with them. They are always going to be trying to pick a fight, and if you simply refuse to argue, eventually they will stop the negative behavior. Stay calm and always use a peaceful tone of voice. A narcissist will always try to talk over you so you will, in turn, raise your voice to get your point across. All this does is escalating things in their favor. When you refuse to get angry, it will be hard for them to use gaslighting phrases against you that will diminish your feelings and your self-worth.

Narcissists will always try to bait you into the position they want you in. They will try and keep you on the defensive by using mean remarks and insults. Know what they are doing and counterattack by staying calm. This can be hard, but it is absolutely possible. When you can find your calm and hold on to it, you will see very quickly how the narcissist will back down. Understand that they will continue to try and get you angry, but you simply must refuse. Eventually, they will get the hint and stop picking on you or leave altogether so they can find a new victim.

Chapter 20 - Divorcing a Narcissist

There is no divorce in the world that is easy; however, divorcing a narcissist can be a very scary time in life. You may be worried about the safety and well-being of not only yourself but also your children. If you have made the decision to divorce your narcissistic spouse, there are definitely some things you need to know. You will need to find help and create a good defense. We will also clue you in on how to deal with a narcissist in court as it is not as cut and dry as other divorce situations.

Many people, after realizing that they are married to a narcissist, find that the best thing they can do for their overall safety and well-being is to divorce them. This is oftentimes the best decision for themselves, as well as their children. Making the decision may be difficult, but at the end of the day, it will be better for not only you but also for your children. It takes bravery and knowledge to venture down the road of divorcing a narcissist.

Divorcing a narcissist can become a real mess. People usually work together to stay out of court and try to find alternatives to the messy process that divorce can entail. When dealing with a narcissist, they will do their best to make things as messy as possible.

While no one really wins in a divorce, the narcissist will strive to feel as if they have won. More often than not, when handling divorce, people simply hope for things to be split down the middle. This includes assets and responsibilities. The narcissist is not going to see it this way at all. They are excellent at playing the victim and will have no intention of trying to meet you in the middle. They will not take the route of mediation or negotiation.

Their goal will be to be the one seen as being in the right. The truth of a narcissist is anything but truthful.

They will go to great lengths to make themselves look good and sway the opinion of everyone, including a judge, to see things from their point of view even if it is tragically skewed.

The narcissist is also a master game player. They have been doing it their whole life, and if you think a courtroom is going to stop this behavior, you are sadly mistaken. In fact, they will likely up their game because they are truly after a win. They love to hold the power, and they do this by keeping other people off-balance. Unfortunately, narcissists tend to be charismatic and charming. This can win favor with a judge or other people involved in your divorce. They will do whatever it takes to wear you down or win the favor of the ones that are making decisions. This makes them dangerous to deal with, especially when kids are involved.

They will use anything and everything against their soon to be ex, regardless of the ill-effect it may have. They will even use the children involved as pawns or strategy for the win.

Most people find the court to be a stressful place that they would rather avoid. This is untrue for the narcissist. They love power and control, and they can find a sense of it while dragging you through a difficult and lengthy court process. They find a thrill in the whole process. A narcissist will not have any care as to how long the process of court proceedings take. In fact, they may even do their best to prolong the experience so they can maintain power and control over you. This makes the stress of divorce even worse. It can really wear you down, but you must stay strong and persevere. They will do everything they can to keep their grip on you and tear you apart. Rely on your friends, family, and lawyer to keep you strong, and you work through the longer than normal process of divorcing a narcissist.

One of the worst things you can do when dealing with a divorce from a narcissist is to throw your hands up in the air and say, "I give up." This is exactly what the narcissist wants. They will go to great lengths to ensure this happens. It not only gives them the win but also enables them to feel good about besting you.

They will use this to their advantage with their "friends" and other people to try and continue to make you look bad and to make them look like the victim. Stay strong.

It is extremely likely that you will end up in court when divorcing a narcissist as they will refuse to converse reasonable terms.

Common Strategy that Narcissists will use in Divorce

There are tons of narcissists in the world, and a lot of research has been done on them and narcissistic personality disorder. When it comes to divorce, they always have a strategy that will help them procure the win.

Being aware of their strategy can help you when trying to counter their moves. You have to remember that this is all a game to them. We are going to look over some of the common strategic moves that a narcissist will make to ensure that they find the outcome they are looking for.

Family court proceedings can take a very long time. This is true in just about every state. When you are dealing with a narcissist, this amount of time is sure to be even lengthier. They will file a ton of motions, even if they are ridiculous, to make everything take more time. This will delay proceedings. They may fake emergencies or make simple requests to put off hearings until a later date. This tactic is used to try and wear them soon to be ex-partner down.

The narcissist will always play the victim. As you know, the truth of a narcissist is theirs alone, and no matter what you say or what the actual truth is, they will only see themselves as right and as the victim.

They may also use tactics like not showing up at a scheduled hearing, providing information to lawyers that are misleading, or keeping information to themselves to try and delay court proceedings. This can beat their partner down and help set them up for the win. The narcissist believes that they are better and smarter than anyone. This makes them assume that their lawyer and the judge will ultimately believe what they have to say. Unfortunately, depending on the narcissist that you are dealing with, this may absolutely be the case.

You should never expect the narcissist in your life to negotiate or settle when working through a divorce. They have an understanding that the longer they can drag things out, the more susceptible you will be to the pressure they put on you. Their ability to manipulate you will be enhanced. They're counting on the fact that you will succumb to the pressure that they put on as it keeps them in control.

The narcissist and their lawyer will make offers that are absolutely laughable. They won't respond to proposals in a timely fashion, and they will stall whenever they see the opportunity. There will be no dealings of good faith. When dealing with a narcissist, you cannot find a middle ground.

They will stand firm in the same position regardless of the facts that are being presented.

You need to maintain your strength and refuse to allow them to beat you down and take control of the situation.

Another part of the reason that the narcissist will try to lengthen the process is to run up the cost of your bills.

Divorce is an expensive process regardless of the person that you are divorcing, but it becomes exponentially pricier when you are dealing with a narcissist. They understand that your finances are being impacted, and if they can make it so that you run out of money, they will again have more control over the situation. They will also be hopeful that running you out of money will lead to you simply giving up and taking them back.

It is very likely that throughout your relationship with the narcissist, they said and did things to make you look bad. This is only going to get worse when you are trying to divorce them. They will say any and everything that they can think of to degrade your character and simply hope that some of it will stick and that people will believe them. They will not take the time to think about how this will affect you or the consequences, and they simply want to win regardless of the cost.

One of the major problems that go alongside this tactic is the fact that you and your lawyer will then be forced to try and defend against it.

This will take more time, which is something the narcissist is always striving for. Additionally, it is going to cost more money. It can also be emotionally devastating. This is especially true when people start to believe what the narcissist has to say. Your lawyer needs to be fully aware of what they are dealing with, so they can count her and ensure that the judge does not fall for the tactics of the narcissist that pollutes the vision of who you truly are.

Another reason that the narcissist will work so hard to destroy your character is the fact that it will gain them more support. It plays into their victim complex and helps inflate their ego even more.

This is a very hard thing to watch when you understand what is going on but take solace in the fact that the people who truly know you and care about you will never fall for this type of degradation and manipulation.

Do your best to not allow the discourteous things that they say about you to throw you off course. Stay strong and focused, and the best outcomes for you and your children and allow the nasty words of the narcissist to roll off your shoulders. The less attention that you pay to the things that they say that are absolutely abhorrent, the less power you put into the hands of the narcissist.

You must also prepare yourself for never-ending court sessions. Even after the divorce is finalized, the narcissist may try and get you back into the courtroom. This is easy to do when there are kids involved. There are a bunch of different moves they can make to put you back into the legal system, and they will use everything and anything they can against you. Be prepared for them to break custody agreements, not pay bills that are due, or even violate your or your children's privacy just to get you back in court.

The process of dealing with a divorce from a narcissist may feel never-ending but know that as long as you stay strong and focused on what needs to happen, eventually, it will all calm down, and the narcissist will likely move on. You need to make sure you have a support network. This can be friends or support groups; even online forums can be very helpful. With support, you will gain more insight into the tactics the narcissist is using and what you can do to keep yourself and your children safe from the toxicity that they spread.

Chapter 21 - How to Choose a Divorce Attorney

Choosing an attorney is difficult. Do you pick the one with the most ads, the best ads, or the one that your friend used?

Do they have the three c's?

Rather than reading ads and only asking your friends about the attorney who helped them "win" their case, interview attorneys and look for those with these three c's—competent, caring, and cost conscious.

Although it may create an initial delay in the filing of your petition and even the payment of multiple consultation fees, if possible, consult with three different lawyers. What you learn about the process and how different attorneys' practice may save you thousands of dollars and a much greater delay if you have to switch attorneys later.

Does the attorney's skill and experience match your need?

A consultation should clarify your divorce options and issues. Does the attorney help you understand ways to resolve your case or are they encouraging immediate litigation? Are they also a mediator? Do they feel as comfortable in the courtroom as they do in mediation? Listen, make notes, and ask questions.

Caution!

If the attorney advises you before you have provided your background information, beware. Not knowing your unique facts and what you are seeking in the divorce may indicate a lack of experience and sensitivity to nuances in divorce matters. It may, on the other hand, just indicate you have found someone with a big ego. In either case, consider consulting another attorney.

As you listen to the attorney's spiel about themselves or their practice, think about how your needs match their abilities and experience. Do they have the experience to handle your divorce?

Competent/Trustworthy

Whenever you hire any professional, make sure you choose one you think you can trust and the one with the level of experience and expertise that you need to present your case. An uncontested matter will generally require less experience and expertise than a contested matter.

Not all attorneys are experts in divorce but not all divorces require an expert. Your attorney's knowledge and experience should when possible, match the level of experience and expertise necessary to complete your matter. However, because some advertise that they practice divorce, but rarely do and others have years of experience but don't advertise themselves as experts, to determine an attorney's experience will generally require that you personally meet and consult with them.

Recent law school graduates may know the law enough to pass the bar exam but may not have the necessary experience to handle a complex divorce. Law school does not teach anyone how to practice. That only comes with experience.

How important are credentials?

Don't let credentials be the only way you qualify an attorney. First, consider the attorney's communication skills. Are they personable and easy to talk to or gruff and arrogant? A gruff, arrogant attorney may be a strong advocate in court or have extensive experience, but if you want an amicable resolution, someone with strong emotional intelligence may be a better choice than even someone who is a bulldog in court.

Many states have certification programs for attorneys to set themselves apart from others based upon their expertise. Very few attorneys are board certified and they generally come with a higher price tag. A board-certified attorney may have initially passed an exam, like a bar exam, in marital and family law and are also required to keep up with changes in family law. However, being board certified doesn't guarantee they are ethical, smarter, or a better communicator. Nor does it suggest they are caring or cost conscious. If a lawyer has years of experience and is caring and cost conscious, choosing one who is "board certified" may not be the best choice.

Questions to ask during your consultation

Do they seem to genuinely care about you and your case? If you are bothered by their "bedside manner" or lack thereof, they may have a reputation in the legal community for being difficult. This is why your observations about the office and staff paired with questions about an attorney's background are crucial.

If the attorney asks for an amount of money in advance to secure his services (retainer) and the amount seems inflated or the attorney instills fear about your case and how much expertise it will take to resolve it—stop, go home and give yourself time to think about their comments. If the attorney bases the retainer on the cost of a trial, and their strategy is "always to go to trial," it may be time for you to do more research about them as well as your ability and willingness to commit to a trial before you have even filed a petition. Most cases settle and it is only the most adversarial that go to trial. The adversarial posture of a case may be the result of the unwillingness of the parties or the attorneys to settle.

If cases go to trial, the divorce is set to last longer than six months and to require multiple hearings and consume much more attorney time than those that settle after mediation. If you have assets including businesses valued at millions of dollars and believe that your divorce will require experts and multiple days of trial, a retainer of twenty-five or fifty thousand dollars may be justified, but retainers are generally nonrefundable. After paying a high retainer and then having your case resolve two days or even a month later during a mediation, may mean you have paid too much or the estimated time and skill to finish your divorce was overinflated.

Remember, this person will be sending you a bill every month. If you don't get along after one hour or there is something that does not seem right, look for a different attorney.

Chapter 22 - When to Tell the Kids About the Divorce

The timing of your announcement is as important as what you'll say about the divorce. You'll be talking about a sensitive topic that will bring up strong feelings for all of you. Planning when and how to best carry it out will help you calm any anxiety you may feel about telling your children this hard-to-hear news and gives you a structure to follow in what is often a very chaotic time.

The first timing issue is how much notice to give before one of you moves out of the house. Depending on their ages, your children will need differing lengths of advance warning. With young children, preschoolers to preteens, my recommendation is to tell them no more than two weeks prior to a parent moving out of the family home. Anything shorter can leave them stressed and overwhelmed, as if things are moving too fast. Anything longer encourages false hope that the divorce won't happen. Teenagers are better able to understand the situation and can handle learning about the separation and divorce up to a month or so before it happens.

The second timing consideration is choosing the actual day and time for your conversation. Here are some things to think about:

BE READY

Choose a time to talk when you feel emotionally prepared. Come with a clear head—no alcohol or drugs for false courage. Stick to a script. Don't blurt out the news just to get it out of the way.

TELL CHILDREN FIRST

Respect your children enough to tell them before you tell others. This is especially important if there is a chance that they could hear the news from someone other than you, like a friend or family member. This is hard news to receive and getting it secondhand makes it even more painful.

CHOOSE AN HOUR OF THE DAY WHEN YOU ARE REFRESHED

Stay away from late nights, early mornings, or talks before bedtime, heading to school, or when you're about to leave for work.

CHOOSE A TIME WHEN YOUR CHILDREN CAN CONCENTRATE

Do your best to avoid times when children are sick, distracted by other events, tired, or hungry.

ALLOW PLENTY OF TIME

Give your children all the time they need to take in this big information. Be open and willing to hear what they have to say and ask if they have any questions or want to say anything.

BE MINDFUL OF SCHEDULES

Avoid important dates like holidays, birthdays, the first day of school, or the first day of summer vacation to name a few. This talk will stay embedded in your children's brains long into adulthood. Try not to link a special occasion to this very emotional experience.

WATCH OUT FOR "HIT AND RUN TALKS"

I coined this term after hearing many stories of parents gathering their children to tell them about the divorce, and then disappearing immediately afterward. The parents would drop a bombshell and then be completely unavailable to a child who might have a question or just need a hug. Schedule your conversation for a time when you're available to stick around afterward. Your presence will provide comfort, even if your children retreat to their rooms.

NO ADVANCE WARNINGS

Telling your children ahead of time that you are going to have a talk about divorce will only increase their anxiety. Simply announce the meeting as you are heading into it.

Things to Avoid in Your Talk

You are about to tell your children that everything they've known and counted on in their family is changing. This is not the time to ask them to agree with your decision or otherwise make you feel better. This talk is for them. To make your conversation as low-stress and productive as possible, stay child-focused. These tips can help:

Avoid interruptions. Turn off all screens: no phones, tablets, computers, or television. Set up a welcoming, emotionally safe environment.

No tattling. This isn't the time to divulge sensitive details about why your marriage isn't working or to try and get the children on "your side." In fact, there isn't ever an appropriate time for this.

Stay away from trash talk about each other. This conversation is going to be hard enough on your children. Subjecting them to a verbal bashing session between their parents will only make it much worse. Be respectful and businesslike.

Watch your body language. Children will read your nonverbal cues as well as the words you use. Try to avoid sitting like an emotionless robot or a volcano about to explode. Make your facial expressions mirror your words. And no smirking, eye rolling, sarcasm, or put-downs.

No runaway emotions. It's good to share your feelings with your children. You may find your voice cracking or tears clouding your eyes as you speak. This is normal and perfectly fine because it helps your children understand how difficult this decision is for you. However, uncontrollable weeping or over-the-top emotional outbursts will frighten your children and make them think they must take care of your emotions rather than their own.

Don't play the blame game. Don't identify one parent as responsible for the divorce. It's better to say that you've made the decision together, and that no one is the "bad guy."

Sidestep the "L-word." When you tell your children you no longer love the other parent, it leaves them worried that you'll stop loving them too. Even gentle, tactful explanations about the differences between adult love and parental love can be confusing. It's much more effective to describe how the relationship has changed. For example, "We argue a lot," or, "We don't agree on many things," or, "We're no longer happy being married to each other." While these can still be confusing, children understand arguments and unhappiness much easier than trying to figure out falling out of love.

Where to Have the Talk

As you plan the setting for your talk with your children, think about what they will need. Choose a location that is familiar, private, and emotionally safe.

FAMILIAR

Your children will probably feel most comfortable in their home. You might sit in the living room or around the kitchen table. Sometimes parents will request the conversation be held at a therapist's office. This only works if the children know and feel comfortable with the therapist. Never schedule an appointment with someone who doesn't know how to facilitate this talk.

PRIVATE

This is a conversation that needs privacy. There are likely to be tears or emotional outbursts that could embarrass a child if overheard. These are normal reactions that we don't want to suppress. Choose a place where you won't be interrupted or worry about who might be listening. This isn't a conversation for a restaurant or other public location. Respect your children's feelings and give them the privacy they need.

EMOTIONALLY SAFE

Familiarity and privacy will go a long way toward helping your children feel safe enough to participate in this emotionally difficult conversation. You should also use what you know about each of your children to meet their individual needs for emotional safety. For some kids this might mean they feel safest when it's just the two of you with your child curled up on your lap on the family room couch, while others might feel safest in their bedroom but want their siblings present.

Chapter 23 - The Information on Rights

Dealing with an ex-spouse is quite tricky and also challenging most of the time because of the strained relationship caused by the separation. Unfortunately, one is without a choice when the matter to deal with concerns the welfare of the children.

One of the problems that divorced couples deal with has a lot to do with exercising their rights over their children. Who has superior rights? What are the limitations? Should they share custody over the children, or will it be better if only one of them have custodial rights? The quick fix that most divorced parents employ is to just compromise so their children can live harmoniously and peacefully with least effect of their divorce.

- Who exactly has the rights over the children?

As parents, both the mother and the father are entitled to have child custody rights over the children. If the courts find that both can provide for a comfortable and stress-free environment for their children, without unnecessary complications, then they can both be granted custodial rights. There are instances, however, when only one parent is awarded such rights due to various reasons such as poor parenting skills, lack of financial support, and abandonment. When this happens, the rights that the neglecting parent may either become limited or in the worst-case scenario, they may be revoked, as suitably determined by courts.

Moreover, in situations where both parents are equally unable to satisfactorily perform their parental duties and obligations, child custody rights can be awarded to relatives such as the grandparents or aunts and uncles of the children, or the family court, will appoint a suitable guardian.

- What is these child custody rights?

There are two basic child custody rights, namely: Physical child custody rights and Legal child custody rights. The former deals with the actual taking care of the children and the daily living arrangements whereas the latter is concerned with parental decisions as regards the children's important life events such as their education, choice of religion, medical care and others.

- How are these rights exercised by both parents?

Most of the time, both rights are awarded to the mother while the father gets to be participated in just the latter. The rationale behind this is that a mother is deemed to be able to care for the children better than the father, especially if the children are still at a young age. But of course, there is an exception to this case such as when the mother abandons her kids or if the family court finds that she is not physically or financially capable to care for them.

- Do the rights exclusively involve the children only?

Although primarily, the rights concern the children only, some of it nevertheless involves one parent. A parent who exercises physical child custody over the child or children has the right to demand support from the other parent. Hence, in some situations, it is not only the children who are being financially supported by the other parent but also the custodial parent who takes care of them.

The most extreme right that a custodial parent has is the right to change the children's names. This is not an ordinary situation and the general rule is that a parent cannot ask for the change in the children's names without the consent of the other, but there are allowances as provided for by the law. In cases where the non-custodial parent's rights are being removed or if the custodial parent just wishes to add her own name, the change can be asked from the family court, subject of course to a hearing and the evidences presented.

- What are some of the rights of the parent having legal child custody only?

As for the parent who only has legal child custody, aside from being able to voice out his opinions and suggestions when it comes to parental decisions, he also has visitation rights. Most family courts award the other parent weekend visitations as to nurture the relationship between the children and said parent. It is very essential that the other parent be given this right so that the children will not feel alienated by said parent and at the same time, such parent can comply with his parental duties despite the separation.

These visitation rights may be modified accordingly to both parties' and their children's convenience. Although this right may sound simple, there are actually many disputes revolving around matters such as when a mother will not permit the father to see his children even in visitation days; or when a father constantly fails to show up on said scheduled dates; or when the parents failed to observe the court-ruled visitation schedule due to their personal issues.

- How are these rights determined?

These rights are usually determined by the court through the proofs of evidence submitted by both parties. Parents who have no trouble getting along usually pass their mutual agreement to the court and wait for approval. But for those who have to battle things out, the court has to go through tons of statements and proofs provided by both parties wherein they shall show how one parent is a better fit for custody or how one parent has poor parenting skills.

These are just some of the basic facts that one should understand about different child custody rights. Parents who are in said situation has to take note that acquiring the rights over the children is not a contest or a competition against one another and it is definitely not about who is the good parent and who is not – it is mainly about the children and what is best for them. Therefore, no matter what the issues are between the parents, it is very important that they work around it so that they could raise their children properly and agreeably.

Chapter 24 - Managing the Trauma of Your Divorce

Divorcing a high-conflict spouse can feel like living in a war zone. You never know when a bomb is going to go off, so you're constantly on high alert. It's important to know how your body reacts to chronic stress, so here's a mini-neurochemistry lesson.

Cortisol levels peak in the morning, to get you out of bed, and decline as the day wears on, so you can fall asleep. Cortisol does good stuff, like helping you to maintain steady blood-sugar levels and fueling your brain. It's also an anti-inflammatory agent that prevents tissue and nerve damage.

When you're under attack—either physically or psychologically—your cortisol levels surge. You need cortisol to give you the energy to cope with stress or flee from actual danger. Cortisol is great in the short term, but sustained release, in layman's terms, can really "f" you up. High-cortisol symptoms include:

• Depression.

• Fatigue.

• Weight gain.

- Back pain.

- Trouble concentrating.

- Low libido.

- Acne.

- Impaired memory.

- Insomnia.

- Irritability.

- High blood pressure.

- Sugar cravings, of the kind leading you to ingest a box of Thin Mints or a whole large pepperoni pizza at one sitting.

Too much cortisol scrambles the body's stress response system, which helps us respond optimally to stressors. If you find yourself overreacting to relatively benign events—for instance, having a panic attack when you hear the ping of an email arriving on your phone—this is a sign of cortisol dumping.

Cortisol dumping is a major player in the traumatic stress associated with divorce. High cortisol levels hijack your brain and cause you to have kneejerk reactions to input instead of having reasonable responses. Classic divorce post-trauma symptoms include:

- Ruminating about your ex's heinous behavior.

- Trouble sleeping and nightmares about your ex.

- Constant jitteriness.

- Mood swings.

- Hypervigilance (always waiting for the "other shoe" to drop).

- Engaging in hostile email and text communication.

- Raging.

- Difficulty with mundane tasks and basic decisions due to being overwhelmed by divorce.

- Feeling numb and disengaged.

Most people going through divorce experience trauma. Your life as you knew it is unraveling, after all. But when post-traumatic divorce stress goes on for more than six weeks, it can become a full-blown disorder, hence the moniker divorce post-traumatic stress disorder (PTSD).

In order to manage divorce PTSD—instead of it managing you—you need to develop trauma resiliency skills. It's kind of like being a dry drunk who, while abstaining from alcohol, still rages as if he were inebriated because he hasn't learned to be emotionally sober.

Trauma resiliency skills involve doing things to regulate your brain's stress response system, so you're in a state neither of hyperarousal (on high alert) nor of hypo arousal (numb and checked out). Here are some basic ways to manage divorce PTSD and restore your nervous system to baseline.

• Set a divorce curfew. Do nothing related to your divorce after 8 p.m. No emailing your ex or your attorney, no preparing legal documents, no rehashing the latest installment in your divorce saga over the phone to friends. Admittedly, there may be times when you have to do divorce stuff at night (say, if you're on a court-imposed deadline). But as a general rule, set your divorce aside so your cortisol levels will drop, and you can get a decent night's sleep.

• Eat sanely. The stress of high-conflict divorce can make it hard to eat. Some people shed weight they don't need to lose because they're too emotionally overwrought to think about meals. Others pack on the pounds by stuffing their feelings with the latest sugary treats from Trader Joe's. Either way, you're throwing your blood sugar levels off-kilter and making it hard for your brain to function. Eating regular, small, protein-rich meals will stabilize your blood sugar and energy. If you gag at the thought of food or find the prospect of preparing it overwhelming, have easy foods on hand, like hard-boiled eggs, nuts, and cheese sticks.

• Practice good sleep hygiene. Sleep deprivation will make everything seem worse. It's like taking the express train to depression and anxiety, especially if poor eating has already compromised your ability to function. Getting a good night's sleep is critical in managing symptoms of post-trauma, so cultivate good sleep hygiene habits: Go to sleep at the same time every night, try to make your bedroom as dark as possible, quiet any racing thoughts by listening to a meditation app or a white noise machine. Program your mind to associate your bed with sleep, so try to do work or watch TV in another room. The blue light emitted from computer and phone screens messes with your melatonin (sleep hormone), so don't look at those in the hour before bedtime. If your sleep hygiene protocol isn't enough to lull you to slumber, consider seeing a doctor for medication. For all those who hate the thought of taking psychotropic medication, you will not win any medals for toughing it out. Taking meds is better than enduring chronic insomnia.

• Exercise. Exercise is nature's mood stabilizer. So much so that psychiatrists usually tell patients with depression and mood disorders to exercise every day. If you can't manage daily workouts, then aim for three to four times a week. You don't have to do anything strenuous; twenty minutes of moderate exercise, such as walking, will do the trick. Another benefit of regular exercise is that it will help you sleep.

• Resourcing. If you've experienced divorce trauma, you may be on high alert most of the time. Things could be going swimmingly, but you're poised for disaster. To be blunt, you freak out over nothing or next to nothing. In order to assess reality accurately and function normally, you need to develop internal and external sources of safety. This is a fancy way of saying you need to identify ways to calm yourself down that do not include drugs, alcohol, sex with the wrong people, or bags of fun-sized candy. Here are two resourcing tools, one internal and one external.

o Grounding is an example of an internal resource that's super easy to do. You simply look around, wherever you are, and focus on one object at a time. Then, either silently in your mind or aloud, you describe in detail what you see. For instance: "That wall clock is round, with a bright red rim, a white face, and black numerals in a modern-looking font." I think it's more effective to do this out loud, but if you're having an anxiety attack in a room full of people, you probably want to do it silently. Grounding is a simple, but powerful tool because it shifts your focus from worrying about the future or ruminating about the past to the present. It's a way of reassuring your mind that you're safe.

o   Seeking support is an example of an external resource. You identify trustworthy people to talk to, or simply to be around, who will help you feel safe. You gain strength from comforting or inspiring people. They could be friends, relatives, a therapist, or a clergyperson. They should not be your children, your cousin Mabel who's still bitter about her divorce ten years ago, or anyone who's prone to catastrophizing. When you seek support from a trusted person, try not to talk endlessly about your evil ex. Retelling your problem story will just retraumatize you, and the goal of resourcing is to shift your focus away from the trauma so you can develop felt states of safety. Share just enough information so your support people understand what's going on. You may not need to say anything at all; being around someone who makes you feel good may be enough.

•   Trauma-informed therapy. For more guidance and support developing trauma resiliency skills, see a therapist who specializes in trauma. A trauma specialist may offer more sophisticated tools, such as eye movement desensitization and reprocessing (EMDR), a protocol designed to alleviate the distress and hyperarousal caused by traumatic memories, and somatic experiencing, an intervention aimed at releasing physical tension that remains in the body after a traumatic event. Trauma specialists prioritize physiological desensitization—

getting less stressed out—over talking. The idea is that you need to be able to calm down and stop reacting to bad memories so you can talk about them without retraumatizing yourself.

• Breathwork. Talk therapy doesn't work for everyone. And I say that as someone who is primarily a talk therapist! Some people need to experience things physically in order to think differently and change their behavior. Breathwork is a breathing technique that helps people work through trauma. It does not depend on conscious thought, so it gets around the defense mechanisms that perpetuate poor choices. For example, the thought: My ex is such an asshole that I'm justified telling him off in an email or wasting an entire afternoon pacing around the house and ruminating about the ways he's wronged me. Breathwork is becoming a popular alternative treatment for addiction, trauma, and other mental health issues. You can find programs offered in Southern California, New York, and Arizona.

Chapter 25 - How to Get Over Them in Real Life

Dealing with the Aftermath

After encounters with a psychopath, one of the most common problems empaths face is their (often accurate) perception of the injustice of how they were treated. We can examine ways to get over the ruin by looking at specific situations, like the following:

'I am recently separated and upset by the unfairness of the entire situation. My ex got the money, a new woman and a happy life, and I am left with nothing. I am emotionally shattered and destroyed. How do I overcome this exceedingly unfair outcome?'

It may seem unbearably unfair on the surface but look deeper. Don't undersell the most valuable commodities that money just can't buy:

Freedom

Time

Inner truth

Don't be jealous of the new partner. She's actually the victim. You are free to do anything now. You can rebuild, with a valuable lesson behind you. It can only get better from this point. At best (if the psychopath loves the new partner in the only way they know how) she will be owned and controlled like a possession and pet, with no freedom to direct her life. Over the long term, it's a psychological prison with dangerous consequences. At worst, the new target will be robbed of her money, trust, sanity, energy and possibly health. She may be completely broken, a shadow of her former self. When she gets out, she's in for at least 12 months of deep recovery. You, now, have everything open to you.

Don't be jealous of him or his life. Psychopaths never learn and they never grow. They are trapped in a losing cycle dependent on the uncertain winds of fate.

Weak foundations – The psychopath has never developed the patience, work ethic and character foundations that result in satisfying rewards. The sad thing is that they never will. Their motto will always be 'immediate gratification of the self', by deception and conning others.

Delusional thinking – Although most psychopaths feel no love and loyalty to anyone, they expect unconditional love and loyalty from those over whom they've established a dominance bond. Anything less is a justification for them to act out. This belief system is delusional. In real life, can such expectations ever result in interpersonal happiness? It's a hopeless, perpetual lose-lose cycle.

Outer image built upon sand – The only way the psychopath can continue their convincing presentation of success is by pulling increasingly bigger scams on unsuspecting targets. Always, underneath the presentation, they are pure, hollow frauds. They can't control or change themselves internally for lasting fulfillment or success, and consequently, their illusory success depends on external factors that are outside of their own control. It's only a matter of time when things catch up with them – typically by offending the wrong powers, being involved in an incident that exposes their backgrounds or mistaking an eagle for a lamb.

Can never feel the nourishment of love, truth, spiritual wisdom – Psychopaths are stuck with being a black hole, eternally empty. They need to constantly fill this hole up with external things, temporary thrills. They will always live somewhat aimlessly, never experiencing a fulfilling life with purpose in their heart, or the soul-enriching quality of love and affection. And in most cases, they contribute very little to the world.

Is this really an enviable way to live?

But you are a rechargeable battery, capable of change. You are capable of building foundations that are the pillars of lasting happiness. And thus, you possess infinite future possibilities in finding love, success and fulfillment.

You may have been robbed temporarily, simply because you didn't know these types of people existed. No matter how shattered you may be, you will recover – you just don't know it yet. You can overcome the temporary setback by taking positive action and moving forward.

It doesn't matter how pretty the presentation is. The core of the psychopath's ethos is a fraud. Once you get over the emotional aspect of the situation, and see their core for what they truly are, they are losers and poor investments for you.

Don't be jealous of their life together. Photographs and constant Facebook updates are just that, illusions. How do we know that's really their reality? It generally takes two healthy people to have a happy relationship. One toxic person and a new, naïve source of supply are not the ingredients that bode well for long-term happiness.

Be glad for freedom. You have time, the most precious resource, free from bondage and unperturbed by toxic individuals. Don't let it go to waste.

Now the question is, what will you do with your freedom, precious time, and new-found inner truth?

How to Establish NCEA (No Contact Ever Again) Strategically

Establishing NCEA in tiered steps or stages works the best. Psychologically, sometimes you need to trick yourself to make sure you adhere to what's best for you.

1. Make a promise to yourself not to establish contact until you are completely over that person, and they have no further power to affect any of your emotions. Think of this as something temporary you must do, not permanent. It may take a couple of months or even years but give yourself the gift to heal unperturbed in the best environment possible. Then take action to focus 100% on your healing and your happiness. Do not attempt any contact until you arrive at a point where your emotions towards the psychopath become complete indifference.

2. Sooner or later, you will be over it. When you are sufficiently distanced from the excruciating dramas, then it's the time to be rational about things.

3. You will likely find the longer you stay away from the toxicity, the more you can allow the sunshine back into your life again – your heart will feel warm, glowing and radiant once again. When you eventually notice this, be sure to record this transition or moment in time. This will help you remember to stay centered and never to allow external influences to destroy your hard-won serenity and happiness.

How to Embrace the Power of Lists

This exercise involves structuring your thoughts about what is often an emotionally loaded, painful topic through writing a series of tailored lists. It is powerful and incredibly therapeutic.

First, it utilizes how our brain naturally converts information. When you write things down, your brain automatically converts the emotionally incomprehensible to become logically comprehensible. However, when you verbalize the past in continuing 'talking about it', you may relive the trauma and emotional turmoil all over again. Detaching and comprehending is one of the first paths to healing.

Second, these lists take your mind off of a toxic past, and onto a new world of unlimited, positive potentials. You will be able to embrace new ideas and endeavors that are now open to you.

The first batch of lists focus on rationality – so as to separate reality from illusion and see the truth with clarity.

1. Make a list of everyone you know personally that you really admire – people of generosity, genuineness, strong moral compasses, substance and courage.; people who are doing amazing, admirable, great things in life. They might be family members, friends, old bosses, or co-workers. Now compare your real-life heroes to the psychopath in terms of character, actions, life goals, and how they make others feel. Would your real-life heroes do what the psychopath did?

This comparison tactic really does work and is quite powerful. The psychopath compared you against everyone else: isn't it time to compare them against your heroes?

When you take your mind away from their illusory persona, and the emotions of the situation, the psychopath comes up as, well, just pretty much scum – disgusting and kind of worthless in comparison to people who deserve respect.

This is how you direct your thoughts from here on in, not through the manufactured persona that created artificial desirability.

2. Write down all the reasons that you miss the psychopath.

3. Write all the reasons that it is better that he or she is out of your life.

The next batch puts the focus back on you – on your happiness and self-improvement. It gives you something bigger to focus on. Your life is worth so much more. It is much bigger than one toxic and temporary situation.

1. Write what you want to achieve, in terms of short-term, medium-term, and long term goals.

2. Write down everything you are passionate about.

3. Write down everything that you are grateful for (family, friends, personal skillsets, past achievements, present enjoyments and so on). During our down time, we don't see the gifts we already have that make our lives wonderful; the qualities that no one can ever permanently take away.

4. What do you love about yourself? Celebrate your good qualities.

Now the last two lists are inner reflections that ensures the lessons learned stay with you for the rest of your life. You may need some time and introspection before you are ready. But once you have the lists down, you will always have a precious reminder to safeguard your personal well-being, values and long-term happiness.

1. Write a list of what attracted you to the psychopath in the first place. Was it looks? Promises of true love. Attention? A need to be needed. A need to feel approval. A desire to reform someone? A fear of being alone? Use this list to understand what is inside of you that made you vulnerable to them in the first place. Get to know yourself so you won't be blind-sided again by a future invader that provides little value.

2. Lastly, make a list of priority qualities before you look for someone new to date. Focus on internal qualities that are important to you. But keep this list to yourself and don't advertise what you are looking for, as a predator can quickly assume that persona.

Chapter 26 - The Golden Rules of Shared and Co-parenting

The golden rules have emerged over time and I offer these below as my personal guidelines for a happy and successful separated parenting structure. They're pretty self-explanatory and hopefully in knowing a little about the way our lives are structured as described above, you can see how it all works.

Golden Rules in Summary

Golden Rule #1 – Each and every action, decision and guiding principle must be based around the needs of the kids and what is best for them.

Golden Rule #2 – The fundamental basis of the shared-parenting arrangement must be structured, repeatable and enduring in its design to allow it to benefit the children (see Golden Rule #1) and to meet the needs of the parents.

Golden Rule #3 – In combination with rigidity and structure, a shared-parenting arrangement must be able to flex as the needs of the child and the circumstances surrounding the arrangement (either short or long term) change.

Golden Rule #4 – Once Golden Rule #1 has been satisfied, it is okay for the shared-parenting arrangement to be designed for the mutual and individual benefit of the parents. Ensure though that it is equally beneficial otherwise resentments and negativity will creep in.

Golden Rule #5 – In agreeing the terms of a shared-parenting arrangement, there must be a consideration of the overall sustainability of the arrangement, and the effects it will have on the quality of life of the kids and the parents. If the terms of the arrangement require excessive compromise, expenditure, travel, or efforts to be made on a long-term basis then it is likely that the arrangement will at some point cease to work for everyone and may ultimately fail.

Golden Rule #6 –The financial terms of a shared-parenting arrangement should always be negotiated, managed and implemented separately from any other financial arrangements associated with the dissolution of the relationship. Treat any on-going payments that are not split equally between the parents as being focused on the kids and maintain this distinction

Golden Rule #7 –Once you have agreed to move forwards with the shared-parenting arrangement, establish it and immediately start living it (or do so as soon as it is realistically viable to). Apply the same approach to other key decisions, changes and in dealing with events that will doubtlessly occur and need to be managed throughout the arrangement. The time for action is always NOW.

Golden Rule #8 – It is advisable to think about a structured way of doing things, to help adapt to and maintain the shared-parenting arrangement, in as much or as little detail as you feel appropriate to yours and your kids' needs. Expect though that your structures and rules may be different from those of your ex, and don't feel pressured to adapt to their way of working. The key thing is that your overall goals, beliefs, aspirations and priorities for your kids are aligned which will ensure that your kids have a consistent parenting experience across both homes.

Golden Rule #9 – Whilst both parents are unlikely to agree on all matters that require a united-front of parenting, the key thing is to agree on the over-arching principles that shape your shared-parenting arrangement. Within this, matters such as expectations for the kids' behavior, your aspirations and goals for them, the freedoms and disciplines you want them to grow-up with and the priorities for their upbringing should be understood and agreed upon by you both.

Golden Rule #10 – Where possible, agree on an approach to presenting a united front that ensures a level of trust and autonomy is given by Mum and Dad to each other to deal with the day-to-day in line with the overarching principles of the shared-parenting arrangement. In addition to this, ensure that you both agree with and understand the means by which you will handle the more serious or complex matters and ensure that you devote adequate time to this process.

Golden Rule #11 – Communication between you and your ex is CRITICAL to the successful maintenance of your shared-parenting. Ensure that you are able to explain matters in a manner and with due consideration, time and sensitivity depending on the issue at hand.

Golden Rule #12 – Both of your children's places of residence should feel like and be treated as their homes. This sense should come about through both places being physically decorated to feel like home, with as few of their possessions following them about as possible to encourage a sense of permanence and belonging at both homes. A few basic principles can be adopted to ensure that the transit of 'things' between homes is kept to a minimum.

Golden Rule #13 – It is imperative that you protect and preserve the sanctity and structure of your shared-parenting arrangement as you would protect your kids themselves. Do not allow yourself to be swayed by others be they friends, family, new partners or acquaintances in terms of being forced to modify any aspect unless it is specifically for the benefit of the children.

Golden Rule #14 – As you enter into new relationships, and indeed as you contemplate any major life changes, ensure that you are being 100% true to yourself and ensuring that you don't waver on the things that are essential to you in living the life you want. Failing to do this will impact upon your happiness as a person, and on your ability to be the parent that you want to be to your kids.

I believe that the Golden Rules are pretty self-explanatory and furthermore they have stood the test of time, in raising our girls from little more than toddlers, up to the age where the eldest is shortly leaving home to go to University. It's the principles within these Golden Rules combined with our commitment to give our kids the best possible upbringing and not one that was second best, that's been responsible for this in my view.

Chapter 27 - Building A Secure, Safe Home Base In A Two-Home Family

Once a divorce is final, and even during the stages of separation, children will become accustomed to living in two homes, one with each parent, and the changes and adjustments that come with it. In time, they will become acquainted with the arrangement, and learn to accept it. In many cases, children grow up with two parental homes and can learn to enjoy the change in pace from one home to the next. To make the transition to this stage easier is important to establish a regular schedule of when to visit or "live" with each parent. In some cases, separated parents live only a few blocks away from each other, making the visitation process seamless, while other scenarios may involve traveling across town, out of city, or state to visit family. Despite challenges that may occur, it's best to establish a regular flow of activity and scheduling, that will make life easier and predictable for them.

Establishing a Residential Schedule

A regular routine of work, school, lessons, family time, appointments, and more are common items on a calendar, and these can be incorporated into a joint family calendar shared between you, your ex-spouse and the children. If the ex-spouse is unwilling to participate, work on a reasonable and agreeable calendar or plan with your kids. Sometimes you may need to rely on the courts to establish the very specific schedule, with times and dates, so there is little or no way your ex can manipulate his/her way into escaping from their duties as a parent, whether they have full custody, joint custody or visitation rights.

Handling Grandparents, Extended Family on Both Sides of the Family

During a separation, the extended family on both sides often get more involved than we may expect. A divorce not only separates two spouses, but it can separate many people related to the couple, causing division, anger, and resentment on one or both sides. Your ex-spouse's parents, siblings, and another family may try to convince you to reconcile or use you as a scapegoat for their son/daughter's narcissistic issues. There may be a mix of feelings and reactions, with some family agreeing with the separation, if they are aware of the narcissistic behavior, or they may be angry or disappointed. Your own family may be conflicted, especially if they have only experienced the "good side" of your ex. When these situations arise, it can be difficult to carry on with your life until boundaries are established, especially when children are young. Setting a boundary with family can be challenging when the odds are stacked against you, and the narcissistic ex-spouse is good at convincing everyone that you are the bad parent, or the one initiating all that negativity. In this case, establish some ground rules, with the help of legal counsel and/or a third party:

- Set clear dates and times when grandparents and other family members may visit. This doesn't have to be etched in stone, and unless the court mandates it, this can be flexible and should be.

- Make a point of setting a boundary with respect to behavior. Insist that they treat the kids well and agree to avoid negative comments about you or other family or friends that support you. In return, you can promise to adhere to this boundary as well, to assure them that you will only speak fairly of them, and not in a negative or condescending way.

- Set goals and milestones. Communicate as often as necessary, but don't give way too much information where it is not necessary. Announcing a child's graduation from junior high or high school is a good example of positive news to share and event to look forward to. Focus only on the positive and steer clear of any gossip or talking about other relatives. If you have engaged with gossip-flavored conversations in the past, put them to rest when dealing with relationships between a separated family.

New Adults in the Child(ren)'s Life, and When One or More Parents Have a New Relationship

Just when children learn to adjust (or are still getting used to) the change involved in a separation, they may face another challenge in living between two parental homes: a new stepparent, or spouse. The nature in which a new spouse is introduced into the family can vary greatly, though it is a shock or major change for children who are adapting to a divorce, and now a new person in one or both of their parents' lives. There are two sides to this topic to consider:

1.   Helping your child(ren) cope with and adapt to a new partner in their other parent's life
2.   Getting acquainted with and adjusting to your new partner when they become a permanent fixture in your (and their) life.

Coping with your Ex-Spouse's new partner

When your ex-spouse dates again, this may not have a major impact on your children, until they begin a long-term relationship. This can raise a lot of concerns for the following reasons:

- Your ex-spouse's narcissist behavior will have an impact on their new spouse
- The spouse may or may not assume some form of parenting responsibility towards the child(ren), either on their own or because of your ex.
- Your child(ren) may become worried that the new spouse will take your place or distract their other parent from them.

When your narcissist ex-spouse brings a new partner into their life, it will inevitably affect your child(ren) and make them feel that their connection to their other parent is compromised. They may also feel compelled to please the new stepparent, so they can remain in favor and not lose any attention from the narcissist parent. With a new spouse or partner providing a source of "supply" and attention to the narcissistic parent, the children are often placed on the back burner, and not given the same attention as before. They may also be required to appease their new stepparent or join them in doing everything possible to seek approval of the narcissistic spouse/parent.

In some cases, the new stepparent may have a way of swaying your child(ren)'s favor, in accordance with your ex's wishes, and to possibly turn against you. They may convince your child(ren) that you're the enemy and try to lure them against you. This may begin in subtle ways by buying them extra gifts or loosening the rules or guidelines you normally establish in your household. This can have a serious impact on your children, especially if they are young and impressionable. If this is the case, keep your line of communication open with your kids, and let them know that you care about their well-begin and their ability to make their own decisions, within reason.

It's challenging enough for kids when they already feel divided between parents, and even more so when the other parent introduces someone into their life that provides them with the narcissistic supply and attention, they need while creating a sense of competition for the other parent's attention. The child(ren) will feel they are now competing with the stepparent for affection from their other parent. If the new stepparent has children of their own, they may preoccupy the ex-spouse's attention, and he/she may use them to compare your kids to them, which can be mean-spirited and make children feel devalued.

What can you do to reassure your kids when they must cope with your ex-spouse's new partner? Acknowledge that there is nothing you can do in terms of who your ex chooses to date or live with, though if you become aware of any mistreatment, you can advocate for your child(ren) and help them when they need to speak up. Encourage them to confide in you, but also be careful what information you share, because your kids may feel they are betraying the other parent by speaking up. If you are concerned about mistreatment, document every incident or suspected incident you know of, including conversations you have with your child(ren). This will help determine what step(s), if any, to take next, which may involve consulting with your lawyer.

Dating again and helping your children to adjust

You're ready to begin dating again, though you remain cautious about who you decide to introduce into your life, considering your ex-spouse. Unlike your narcissistic ex, you're not going to make a trigger decision to date the next person who pays attention to you, nor will you invite just anyone to become a part of your children's lives and yours. When you begin dating, it's best to approach your new love interest carefully and give them realistic expectations based on your life and your child(ren). Before you introduce them to your kids, prepare your children and your new partner beforehand:

- Your children will need to know that you love them, regardless of who you date, even if you choose to re-marry or engage in a new long-term relationship. They need to know that they come first, and always will.

- Explain to your new partner that your child(ren) occupy a significant part of your life, and always will. It may also be helpful to highlight some of the challenges with your ex, without getting into too much detail, as this can be overwhelming. It's best to limit the contact they have with your children at first, and over time, they will become acquainted with each other over a meal, sports events, or other activities that provide an opportunity to interact in a positive manner.

- Children will naturally feel displaced when there is a new person in your life, especially when they become a regular fixture, and move into the home. They will become a stepparent, whether they assume this role completely or not. Children will expect that the new spouse will occupy more of your time, which may encourage them to see the other parent, either on their own or with some persuasion with the other parent.

Keep your communication with all concerned parties open, which includes more than your child(ren) and your new spouse. Your parents and other family members will need to know about these new changes, so they can become familiar with your new partner. It's important that your ex-spouse knows enough about your new partner, though tread carefully; chances are they will become envious and view the new family member as a threat. There is often nothing you can do to prevent this, except to remain calm and civil concerning custody and visitation arrangements.

Chapter 28 - 4 Ways to Improve Co-parenting

Adjust Your In-Person Communication Style

In every divorce there is a breakdown of communication. Often the divorce happens because of a lack of communication but in some divorces, communication starts to fall apart after the breakup. Just about every set of co-parents has communication problems.

To solve a communication problem, you must realize that the way you are currently communicating is not working and resolve to change that.

If you and your ex are civil enough to try to work through some of your issues together, it can be helpful to think together about communication breakdowns. This is not a chance for finger pointing but is instead an opportunity to shine a light on what is not working.

Here are some basic rules for communication.

Give the other parent information that you would want to know. This is the easiest rule of thumb to rely on. You don't have to try to decide what the other parent wants or needs to know. You don't have to try to evaluate why things you've shared in the past were ignored. Stop trying to make sense of your ex. If it is something you as a parent would want to know about your child, tell the other parent. Do so even if you get no response or a response that you find lacking or inappropriate. Follow this rule and you will go a long way towards keeping communication open and clear.

Keep things brief and on point. Share everything that needs to be shared without elaboration, adding your opinion, or trying to get the other parent to agree with what you think. If your goal is merely to share information (such as the date of your child's concert or what the doctor said at the last appointment), simply do that.

Be polite. This sounds simplistic but it is such an important tip. Remaining polite stops all kinds of problems from developing or worsening. You might not feel like doing it, but politeness may very well be the best way to keep the peace.

Make requests instead of demands. Making this change can be a true turning point. You can still ask for the same things, but how you word it changes, yet you achieve a better outcome. Instead of saying "You need to Sammi's asthma medicine with her," say "Could you send Sammi's asthma medicine with her?" This change in wording makes a huge difference in tone and shifts your positioning in the relationship.

Eliminate extraneous conversation. Keeping conversations centered around what you need to share and not including anything else will keep your conversations focused and on track. It also makes it much harder for your ex to go off the rails and cause an argument.

Change Your Reactions

One of the biggest problems in Co-parenting communication is actually how you yourself react to the communications. Let's be clear here though: you should change your reactions, but you don't need to change your feelings. If your ex says something that really pushes your buttons, your feelings are completely valid, real, and accurate. But that doesn't mean you have to share your reaction with your ex. Instead of firing back, remain quiet or offer a brief remark to conclude the conversation. Go ahead and react to the comments to anyone and everyone else (except your kids!). If you can keep yourself from fighting fire with fire, soon there will be no fire burning. If your ex doesn't get a rise out of you, he or she will likely be forced to tone things down.

Here are some tips for handling reactions that are not helpful:

Anger. This is often the most common reaction when dealing with an ex. He or she does or says things that really gets your goat and you feel that fury rising up in you. You want to yell or shout or do something hurtful. Instead, look at your anger objectively. Yes, you're rightfully angry. But you don't need to let your ex force you into expressing it. In fact, not giving him or her the pleasure of seeing you react can be a wonderful way to "win" in the moment.

Spite. Similar to anger, spite is when you do something just stick it to your ex, like "forgetting" about a change in the parenting plan. Sometimes it feels really great to exact revenge, but that only lasts for a moment and in the long run it causes more trouble. So go ahead and plot your revenge, but just don't actually act on it. You'll get almost as much satisfaction.

Superiority. There are bound to be moments where you want to tell your ex exactly what he or she is doing wrong and why. It can be really tempting to step in and just point out how he or she is screwing everything up. You can rest assured your ex isn't going to listen to you and will probably do the exact opposite of what you see as the perfect solution. Instead, keep your suggestions to yourself and let your ex take the wrong path. Your ex will have to live with the consequences which may be the best revenge.

Coldness. Coldness can be helpful in some situations because it allows you to keep your raging emotions bottled up inside, but aggressive coldness is only going to make things worse. Instead, aim for a neutral tone whenever possible.

Separate Your Personal Relationship from Your Parenting Relationship

When you live together, your lives are intertwined in so many ways. Your relationship and your parenting are all one big jumbled ball. Once you are separated and parenting apart, it's time to tease those raveled strands apart. You have to create a solid yellow line down the road with your relationship with each other on one side and your relationship as parents on the other. The personal relationship side of the road can be filled with U-turns, squealing brakes, swerves, impacts and road rage while the parenting side of the road has to be two hands on the wheel, driving in a straight line at all times.

It can be very challenging to separate these two.

Follow these tips.

Never talk about parenting matters while talking about other problems (like alimony or dividing things up). You have to truly set up separate areas in your brain and keeping these conversations separate will help. It can be helpful to schedule different conversations for different times.

Remember that when you are Co-parenting, you are talking to your child's other parent, that person your child loves and adores. You're not talking to the person who cheated on you, disappointed you, hurt you, or left you. In your mind, talk only to the other parent, NOT the cheater or loser. It can help to almost create two personas in your mind that you have to interact with.

Deal with your emotions. Separating these two relationships does not mean you should suppress your emotions or not cope with them. In fact, the opposite is true. You must work through everything you are feeling about your ex as a co-parent and as your ex-partner.

Keep Your Child Out of It

It sounds funny to say you should keep your child out of your Co-parenting relationship but doing so is one of the most important things you can do to benefit everyone. Your child should not be part of or within earshot of your adult conversations about the parenting plan, parenting issues, or parenting concerns.

Never ask your child to carry messages to the other parent. This is a very easy trap to fall into. "Tell your father I'm going to be late picking you up." "Tell your mother I haven't gotten the child support check yet." As straightforward as these messages seem, they are loaded with emotional undertones. The anger, annoyance, and frustration that is felt by the parent sending the message as well as the emotional reaction by the parent receiving the message are transferred to your child. Your child doesn't understand the nuances of the problem, but he or she knows that both parents are upset, and it can feel as though that anger is directed at the child. Your child will internalize all of those negative emotions and somehow find himself to blame. That is a lot of heavy, adult emotion to place on your child. Find ways to communicate directly with each other.

Don't talk about the other parent in front of your child. This is one of the most commonly recited Co-parenting rules, but it can be the most difficult to put into practice. This means not only should you not speak poorly about the other parent TO your child, but you should also not speak badly of the other parent within earshot of your child. Even if your child is in the same room watching TV while you are talking to a friend, he or she can hear you. And don't try to talk into code, spelling out your ex's name or referring to him or her as "that certain person" or another disguised name. Your child is going to figure out what you are saying. As hard as it is, you goal is to let your child be in a vacuum when it comes to your reaction to your ex. You want your child to maintain a healthy, separate relationship with your ex without your own reactions clouding things. If your ex is a miserable person, your child is going to discover this on his own.

Don't try to guide your child's emotions. There is also a fine line that comes into play when you and your child talk about the other parent. Your child is going to tell you things that happened while with the other parent, offer opinions and emotions, and ask you questions. Strive to be available for your child for all of these kinds of talks but be careful that you are not even subconsciously trying to guide your child into sharing your feelings about the parent. While it's ok to ask "So how did you feel when Mommy forgot to pick you up from practice?" it's not ok to coach your child into having a reaction: "I'll bet you were really mad at Mommy when she forgot to pick you up."

Chapter 29 - Respond Only to Your Ex When It's Necessary, Do Not Respond When It's Not

Victims of abuse have a difficult, long walk to recovery in every way. The trauma of abuse by the person who is supposed to love you the most is life altering. Throw in shared children and the current court climate of cooperative parenting, and victims have an uphill journey to get back to a normal life and emotional stability.

Your abuser, unless he has been through a lot of therapy and has shown you a long pattern of respect and understanding, probably doesn't care about your bruised and battered walk. In fact, to many abusers, narcissists in particular, your pain and suffering makes them feel powerful and in charge. The more vulnerable you are, the more attractive you are to use as a pawn in an abuser's need to dominate others.

I think of it this way: An abuser can be like a vortex in the middle of the lake, sucking in everything that comes its way. The vortex doesn't care if it sucks in a fish, a leaf or a boat full of people. It just continues to spin around and around taking in everything in its path.

An abuser, I believe, may not really care who he dominates on any given day, just that he has had the rush of the feeling as often as possible. Some even believe they are addicted to it.

When you get near your abuser, either figuratively or literally, you are in danger of getting sucked into his vortex. If you are feeling weak that day or he sees you as vulnerable, then you become easy picking.

It took me a long time to understand this and I often assumed that the exchanges between my ex and myself blew up or spiraled out of control because of a miscommunications or misunderstanding. I would replay the event over and over in my head trying to understand just what happened that led to such a mess.

When my husband first put his hands on me so many years ago, I couldn't believe it. In the years that followed, I could never understand why he did that and introduced violence into our marriage. I was sitting in a rocking chair, nine months pregnant, no threat to anyone, no reason for him to charge and begin to squeeze my neck.

It made no sense to me.

When I began to research domestic abuse, I read in many places that statistically, abusers introduced physical violence into the relationship first when their partners are pregnant. Ok, our situation fit the norm. I still couldn't understand why. I didn't understand why he attacked me, a big, exhausted pregnant woman with no ability to hurt him.

Finally, it clicked in my therapist's office. He attacked me that day because I wasn't a threat to him. I was an easy target in order to get that rush of dominance he sought. I didn't know that abusers are always trying to dominate others in order to feel good about themselves. It doesn't mean that in every relationship they are dominating. Sometimes they look for sympathy instead or find the rush in being the "go-to" guy who people admire. Dominating others brings abusers pleasure. It fulfills for them a basic need.

Abusers often see people differently than you and I. Abusers see people as things. And they pay attention to how those things make them feel. The psychology is deep and multi-layered but, in the end, abusers are unpredictable and dangerous. It is best to stay away.

We can't fix them or say the right thing that will bring out the best in them. Oh, maybe for a minute, but it can take lots of exhausting and dangerous effort to achieve even the slightest glimpse of kindness from an abuser when he wants to be dominating.

However, if you disconnect from an abuser and he doesn't want you to, that evil, hurtful man in your life, can become a saint right before your eyes. Abusers can't stand to lose an object that they can control, so they can use faux kindness to bring you back in. Beware, it is not likely to continue and abusers can just as quickly flip their behaviors to dominating jerks all over again.

There is so much information out there about narcissists and the mindset of a domestic abuser. As I said earlier, it is in your best interest to learn as much as you can about the dynamics of this type of person. I don't recommend ever trusting your abuser again, no matter what he is offering.

Instead, it is best for your own recovery to set the goal of "No Contact." This is the term used to describe the strategy used to get a narcissist out of your life and give you a chance to heal.

No Contact mean absolutely no contact of any kind. No emails, phone calls, social media posts or shares, no messages, no acknowledgment of him at all. Not even eye contact when you are in the same room together.

Experts say that No Contact gives the victim the best chance of healing and if maintained by the victim for a certain length of time, the abusers will eventually stop seeking the emotional high from dominating you and move on, unfortunately to other people.

Psychologists advise that when dealing with an abusive narcissist, there are only two choices: 1. Stay engaged and put yourself in harm's way or 2. Stay away from him for good.

No Contact is not easy to pull off when you share children together, especially young children. As a victim of abuse, you know when the court awards unsupervised time to your abuser, you are often anxious about the time your children now have alone with the person who was willing to abuse you. Maintaining contact gives you the ability to react if anything goes wrong.

You may also have a small amount of influence over his actions with the children if you maintain a connection, however fragile and difficult. For years, I was able to do that. I felt more secure pretending to be friends with my ex than actually showing him how much I disliked him. That faux friendship enables me to be there for my kids if anything went wrong and they needed help.

Too often mothers are painted as overbearing and unwilling to let well-intended dads take care of their children. That may be true in some cases, but victims of domestic abuse know all too well that life with an abuser can be truly dangerous.

I wasn't hovering around my children when they were with their dad. By staying friendly with him, I was informed of things in real time and could react to things as needed. One time, while my young son was with his dad, he called me at the end of the day to tell me about school. He told me that he didn't feel well and had a headache. I asked him why and he told me that he fell off the merry-go-round at school and hit his head. He told me how he had to sit out the rest of recess and felt like he was going to throw up.

I asked him to put his father on the phone and then told my ex that he needed to take our son to the hospital because these were symptoms of a concussion. My ex told me he knew about the fall and wasn't worried and I was making too much about it. I was surprised by these reactions because as a sportswriter covering the NFL, my ex knew the dangers of concussions. But he would not be swayed to act. So, I called the kids' pediatrician and set up a conference call with my ex. After going down a checklist with us, the medical professional told us our son need to go to the ER right away.

My ex was still hesitating. So, I said while still on the conference call, that I could drive over to take our son to the hospital and the doctor said that would be a good idea. I asked my ex if he planned to come to the ER too or stay home. He said he would follow us in his car. After the CAT scan, the doctor instructed us that our son had to be awakened every few hours and my ex agreed to let me take him home in order to keep watch.

I didn't understand at the time why my ex was so insistent that it was no big deal. Maybe he had other plans that night that he didn't want to interrupt with a trip to the ER. Maybe he was embarrassed that he hadn't called the doctor himself. Maybe making me look hyperbolic to the children made him feel good. But, using our child's health in this way wasn't acceptable and I am glad that our "friendship" enabled me to get our child the medical attention he needed.

However, staying connected to an abuser comes with great costs. First, it is exhausting because abusers don't make a lot of sense, are unpredictable, scary and often point fingers when it's time to take responsibility. In the worst case, they can cause their victims real physical, emotional and financial damage.

As my children have grown into adults, I have transitioned to the "No Contact" approach and feel that it has been a benefit to my emotional health. I have also come to understand that my children are learning from this as well. Of course, it sucks that they don't have me to rush them to the hospital if they hit their heads, but they are also learning what to do for themselves. They are learning how to manage their own relationships with their parents. These are important lessons for any child, but maybe more so for children of abusers.

No matter what anyone tells you, abuser abuse because they want to, and they can. People don't cause other people to abuse. They are not emotionally healthy. They may never hit their children, though the majority of them do, but they can emotionally hurt their children in many ways. Children will never truly be protected from the pain of having an abuser for a parent.

We can only help them process it and learn to live with it in much the same ways we do.

My children see me set my boundaries and, in every relationship, a certain degree of respect is required, or I am moving on and shutting down the relationship. In other words, they see that there are consequences for abuse. I am hoping that they will never see abuse as acceptable and will never tolerate it.

No Contact gives me the space I need to heal from those slings and arrows he throws that get through and touch my heart.

I have set up artificial boundaries that help me keep my distance.

Chapter 30 - Mistakes Parents Make When Communicating with Their Co-Parent

- Losing your temper

When no longer partnered together it is easy to let stubbornness or resistance set in. Some of the things that "hook" us in conflicts are brought up to causing the other person to get angry. Remember to set aside emotions so the sole focus of your new co-parenting relationship is on your child(ren). If you find yourself persistently being "hooked," you might seek out and join a parenting support group.

- Making it more about the power struggle than the children

Sometimes we are blind to our own motives and behaviors. The other parent may make a request that deviates from the Plan, so we justify our inflexibility and refuse to accommodate their request, even when we would have been flexible to anyone else. Or, we offer the other parent an impromptu visitation time, knowing their work schedule could not accommodate. We convince ourselves of being generous, while the other parent is repeatedly not accepting the terms of our generosity.

Another power struggle is by engaging the children in a behavior contrary to the other parent's values such as taking the child(ren) to events that are not age appropriate or against the other parent's moral values. This undermines the authority of the targeted co-parent by teaching the child the other parent's wishes are not to be respected.

Playing power games with our co-parent can be detrimental to your child's future choices by teaching them that authority figures are not be respected. Children eventually see through the games and lose respect for the parent who played them.

- Using your child as a messenger or asking your child to choose sides

The intact family would not expect the child to be the messenger of important things between the parents, but we thoughtlessly put that responsibility on the child in a co-parent situation. The problem being the impact it places on the child. When a child becomes the messenger, they are exposed to each parent's reaction to the news. They end up the recipient of unpleasantness that is meant for the other co-parent.

This is a common mistake of even the most well-meaning co-parents. It is natural to allow our children to relay communications to their teachers, so

in-turn it seems justified to do the same with co-parents. However, there is an existing emotional attachment shared by co-parents, unlike that of teachers.

- Fighting or criticizing the other parent in front of your child(ren)

This requires great personal restraint, especially if arguments happened in front of your children when your family was intact. And when you still harbor resentment for your co-parent's behaviors, it is easy to lash out in front of the children, especially if you know this would hurt the other parent. Remember your attitude controls your behaviors. Practicing restraint is like building a muscle. The more we practice overriding emotional attitudes with responsible behaviors, that ability to show restraint will get stronger. Eventually we will not get "hooked" by the impulse to criticize each other in front of the child(ren).

Parental Alienation (aka. Hostile Aggressive Parenting)

Even mental health professionals unfamiliar with Parental Alienation can misinterpret a child's disclosures. The fact is a child in an abusive situation has a natural instinct is to protect their abuser. Therefore, when a child is caught in the middle of a high-conflict custody situation, it is crucial for the professionals involved to understand these concepts. Hatred is not an emotion that comes naturally to a child, it is taught.

How to Avoid Making These Co-Parenting Mistakes

- Know your triggers

Note down things that you find upsetting. Maybe it's being late for child exchanges or the child's belongings not being returned. Maybe it's the eye-rolling of the other parent or the snide comments imbedded in conversations. Once you have identified the specific things that trigger you, be mindful of your responses and choose to lighten your reactions.

Have a strategy for when things don't go as planned. In this "contract" include a plan of action for when one parent breaks the rules. This gives each parent permission to hold the other one accountable. The most important thing to remember is, compromise. Everyone slips up once in a while.

• Apologize

An apology is the most powerful tool in a co-parent's toolbox. A sincere apology can bring a fresh start to any relationship. There is a right and a wrong way to exercise the art of apology. First, it is crucial to take ownership of your contribution to the conflict. What did you do? What did you say? How did this impact the other person? No justification for your behavior is to be included in the apology. (i.e. I only said mean things to you because of the way you treated me. So, I'm sorry.)

A sincere apology is powerful. Remember that you are only 'fessing up to your sins. This is not to be approached as an expectation of equal contribution. If your apology comes with the expectation that the other party lay their confessions on the table, then you have not authentically and sincerely apologized.

Chapter 31 - What's Best for the Children?

Your children are the innocents during your divorce process, and they should be protected at all costs. They are incapable of processing what is seen and heard from the most important people in their lives. Children will often feel that they are the reason for their parents separating and divorcing, so it becomes vitally important that we talk with them based on their ages. It can be difficult working with your children if you are in the middle of an emotional breakdown and you are unable to care for yourself when devastated by a divorce.

This is the time to call on all of your immediate support figures, family members, and friends. Perhaps your mom, dad, sister, or a friend can come to stay with you for a while to support you with the children. If no one is available, hiring someone temporarily is another good option. Perhaps there is a good neighbor who can assist you for a few hours a day. Be willing to do what you must to ensure that your children are not suffering and experiencing any emotional or physical harm as you and their father are figuring out how to restructure your new lives apart. What's vitally important is that you take care of yourself and make sure you are well, mentally and emotionally. If you are not taking care of yourself, you will not be able to give your children all the good nurturing, love, and support that they need as their nuclear family unravels.

Depending on the age of the child, they will not be aware of anything that is going on, but small children do need love and nurturing while you work through the difficulties of divorce. Infants and toddlers may not know exactly what is happening, but they can understand security, consistency, love, and nurturing. It is important to reassure our young ones by hugging them often and speaking with them in calm tones and maintaining a consistent routine so that their sense of security is not disturbed.

Preschoolers and young school-age children may understand the word "divorce," but they are more interested in some of their primary needs and have questions like:

Where will I stay?

Am I going to be left alone?

Where will my stuff be?

When will I see Mom?

When will I see Dad?

Do you still love me?

They are more interested in knowing why you are getting a divorce, and over time the questions may become more challenging. Do your best to be honest and share information in a way that is appropriate based on the child's age. How to answer questions about what to tell their friends will require some assistance from you so that they are able to respond in a manner that is helpful for them with their peers.

For school-age children, it is good to explain what is happening in a manner that they can understand. Let them know that Daddy and Mommy are going to be living in separate houses. Reassure them of how much both of you love them. Answer any questions that they may have that may come up in the coming days or weeks. Be sure not to speak ill of the other parent and continue to reassure them of how much they are loved.

Teenagers will generally want the most information and an honest answer should be given but with limited detail. It would be inappropriate to give children the details of what has taken place between you and your husband during the marriage. Always remember that they are your children and not adults and not your friends.

One of the challenges mothers will face is inconsistency with child support. I highly recommend working with the court systems to receive any financial support you should receive from your ex during and after the divorce. Going through the courts is not an attack against anyone; it is a security system you can put in place to ensure you receive financial support for your children. Your children deserve to have the lifestyle they've known maintained as much as possible. If your spouse was the major wage earner and the children will live with you the majority of the time, the financial support or medical insurance should be determined immediately or as soon as possible. If you were the major wage earner and financial support is to be given to your ex for the children, do what is right for the children, even if everything within you does not want to give any money to him. Remind yourself that this is for the children, so that they can be cared for as well as possible when they are away from you.

If you have to give spousal support to your ex, based on the financial calculations that are determined under the law, try to remain reasonable and work within the guidelines of the law and provide the amount that you are legally required to pay. I know this may be difficult for many women, but these are the laws that have been put in place to protect and do what is fair for all. The majority of the time, men are responsible for the child and spousal support during separation and divorce, and we expect them to step up and do what they should. On many occasions they hate that they have to give what has an amount that has been determined by law, so it becomes a huge battle in court to get what the spouse and children are entitled to receive. Some women walk away and just give up. Be strong and do what is best for you and your children.

Conclusion

Whereas Narcissism is all about self-doubt and negative impact, in reality, narcissism is all about inflated self-regard and dressing table. Though narcissism isn't thought to be a cardinal characteristic in conventional notions of personality, it's significant significance in the progression of a nutritious self-concept, such as the human image. We are living in a culture in which reality tv dominates evaluations, and societal media enables all to publish their most romantic, and many inane, ideas and actions. Within this circumstance, it's not surprising the narcissism has enjoyed a resurgence of attention from amateurs both as a kind of psychopathology in its intense form and as a flexible quality of personality when shown in moderation. Clinical psychology will depict narcissists as egocentric, qualified, manipulative, and demanding admiration from other people, whilst personality psychology perspectives narcissism as a standard and beneficial trait related to leadership, assertiveness, self-assurance, as well as the conclusion. Common to both viewpoints though, narcissists believe themselves to be especially 'unique' and they generally pose as very optimistic and at times overconfident in their intellect, ability, and beauty.

In connection to the purpose of the behavior, narcissists' hypersensitivity to gripe and demand for respect are viewed as coping mechanisms made to ward off risks to underlying brittle self-esteem. On the other hand, the obvious paradox that narcissism may be both adaptive and maladaptive might be about level since it's all about kindness. That's, we all know that looking at ourselves through the lens of rose-colored eyeglasses is valuable to great health and well-being but becomes more problematic when those perspectives become too much detached from reality, and also eventually become intense and rigid.

Narcissists do not really adore themselves. In fact, they are driven by pity. It is the idealized picture of these, they convince themselves that they embody, they respect. But down deep, narcissists feel that the difference between the façade they reveal the planet and also their shame-based self. They work hard to prevent feeling that pity. To fulfill this gap narcissists, utilize harmful defense mechanisms that ruin relationships and lead to pain and harm to their nearest and dearest.

Even though many specialists concentrate on the narcissist, I like to concentrate on you as well as the lessons that you want to understand so which you're able to go ahead, proceed, and never replicate the experience. Before you're able to move on, the most essential point to comprehend about narcissists is that under their obvious self-confidence is a deep absence of self-esteem. To prevent entering a different relationship according to your own self-doubt, ask yourself: How do I treat myself better? How do I prevent sending out signs that I want a savior or even a great deal of attention? Nip it in the bud by thinking about yourself. Then you won't attract somebody who places a fantastic potential partner on account of your reduced self-esteem.

If you're beating relationship a narcissist, remember that: you're a sound, real person and likely more effective than you permit yourself to think. Narcissists are all picky. They do not date just anybody. The Search for powerful, accomplished Men and Women who are Pleasant enough to allow the narcissist's self-created superiority overshadows them. In case you've permitted a narcissist to prey in your deficiency of self-confidence, cease! No longer downplaying that you're. It is time to climb into the surface. The lesson This is that you're far better than you believe you are. Adopt the facts and Proceed!

I wish you the best and I am sure that you will be able to overcome this difficult moment and when you have done it you will rediscover yourself a better person, more beautiful, more intelligent and stronger, all this only because you have gained confidence in yourself and have started to see yourself for who you are and not for what you think you should be.

Printed in Great Britain
by Amazon

75507707R00132